I0794811

MODERN DRUMMER® *Legends*

PETER ERSKINE

For access to the digital files referenced in this book,
go to moderndrummer.com/mylibrary

Enter Code
OW8SOP-L5YUFA-N4BDXK

Modern Drummer Publisher / CEO - **David Frangioni**

President - **David Hakim**

Director of Content / Editor - **Mark Griffith**

Senior Art Director - **Scott Beinstock**

Music Transcription - **Terry Branam**

Editorial - **Michael Finkelstein**

Archivist - **Felipe Laverde**

Cover Photo by Marco Soccoli
Back Cover photo by Roberto Ciffarelli

Published by:
Modern Drummer Media, LLC.
1279 W Palmetto Park Rd
PO Box 276064
Boca Raton, FL 33427

Modern Drummer always strives for the best possible content available.
There may be some photos in this issue that do not meet our highest standards.
We have included them for their historical significance, rarity, and importance.
Peter was kind enough to share these photos with us, and we wanted to share them with you.

- CONTENTS -

3 **Foreword**
4 **Introduction**
6 **Peter Erskine: The Doctor Is In**
30 **The Downloads**
30 "Drum Solo" with Stan Kenton
31 Transcription: "Peter at Age Nine Solo"
32 "Cats and Kittens," "Boogie Shuttle Stop," "Hawaii Bathing Suit," "Furs on Ice."
34 **Looking Back**
34 1978, A New Horizon
40 1983, On The Cover
62 1987, On The Cover
80 1993, A Work in Progress
90 2016, Playing With Intent
100 **Equipment**
102 Gear Talk
104 **Photo Gallery**
104 Peter and Weather Report
112 Peter Erskine: The Early Years
114 Peter and Friends
118 Peter and Family
120 **The Songs**
122 **Transcriptions**
Peter's Thoughts On…
123 "Black Market"
124 "Peter's Solo"
124 "Peter's Drum Solo, Osaka 1978"
126 "Fast City"
119 "Sightseeing"
129 "Pools"
130 "Know Where You Are"
132 "Searching, Finding"
136 "Reza"
138 "Liberty City"
140 "Ellis Island"
142 "Samurai Hee Haw"
145 "Esperança"
148 "Cats and Kittens"
149 "Hawaii Bathing Suit"
151 "Boogie Shuttle Stop"
152 "Leroy Street"
154 "Mr. Phonebone"
156 "Furs on Ice"
157 "Friday Night at the Cadillac Club"
157 "Erskoman"
159 "But is it Art?"
160 "The Aleph"
161 "Some Skunk Funk"
162 "Babe of the Day"
164 **Peter Erskine Photo Gallery**

- FOREWORD -

Dear Reader,

This book is about me … at least on its surface.

But, digging just a bit deeper than simply cataloging who I've played with or what brand of drums I use should reveal not only a history of modern American music from the 1950s onward, but a good case study for the "nature versus nurture" paradigm. Not so much a chicken and egg dichotomy, but an exploration of the "tabula rasa" or blank slate described by the English philosopher and empiricist John Locke. If I'm allowed to think of myself as a good drummer, then: are good drummers born? Or are good drummers taught to be, well, "good"?

So, yeah, this book is about me. It is, however and more accurately, about music education in the United States and the state of the entertainment industries, musical instrument development, jazz music and jazz musicians and how everything collided in the early 1960s (the same time I was beginning to get pretty good on the drums).

Music informed my every moment. Perhaps I sought it out, but it was easy to find back then. I'm not talking YouTube-easy, but every radio station or television program did use jazz to sell their shows to America. Jazz was everywhere, it seemed. I learned to speak the vocabulary because I was immersed in the language. My nature was to be curious. But life nurtured me… along with my family and a long list of jazz musicians and educators who paid it forward time and again.

One of the first albums my father or teacher got for me when I was six years old was "Movin' In," by the New York studio drummer and percussionist Specs Powell. The next albums were Art Blakey's "Drum Suite" and "Gretsch Night at Birdland." Soon after I attended my first summer jazz camp which was held on the campus of Indiana University during the summer of 1961 where I met, among others, Louis Hayes and the members of the Cannonball Adderly Sextet. Other mentors at subsequent camps included Donald Byrd, Oliver Nelson, Ron Carter and Alan Dawson. These four men were my friends as well as my teachers. Meanwhile, my listening library was brimming with albums by Max Roach, Miles Davis, Sonny Rollins, John Coltrane, Elvin Jones, Jimmy Smith, Charles Mingus, Shirley Scott, Dizzy Gillespie, Roy Haynes, Roland Kirk, Wes Montgomery, Milt Jackson, Duke Ellington, Count Basie, Herbie Hancock and Thad Jones (in addition to Stan Kenton, Stan Getz, Gene Krupa, Buddy Rich, Dave Brubeck, Gary Burton, Gary McFarland, Cal Tjader, Mike Mainieri ... and Leonard Bernstein!). All to enumerate that my first musical heroes were, and remain, the black artists whose genius developed and produced this unique American art form that would bring the greatest respect and accolades to this country, as well as the greatest joy and meaning to this young drummer. There was never any question in my mind of who created this music.

My musical education continued apace. My parents sought out the best instruction they could find. I can't count the number of doors that were opened for me. Now, I was fortunate to also have been born with a cheerful heart, and there's no doubt that my enthusiasm matched my thankfulness as well as good manners. What I'm trying to say is that I'm certain that my respect and love for these men was apparent enough to them. Still, the amount of good luck and their good will astonishes me and I've never taken it for granted.

I meditate and I pray gratitude for my good fortune and I wish it for every person who hears the call of the drum. May your families and loved ones provide you with even a fraction of the support I received from my own … you will be blessed. And to all of my mentors, colleagues and friends: THANK YOU. In addition to everything else I've learned, I can tell the reader this: whatever your level of involvement might be with drumming, music will ALWAYS be there for you.

– ***Peter Erskine***

P.S. My thanks to interviewers Mark Griffith and Rick Mattingly, as well as to Jon Krosnick, David Hakim and the team at Modern Drummer.

- INTRODUCTION -

For the last 40 years, I have been a *Modern Drummer* reader, and for the last 30 years, I have been a professional drummer and private drum teacher. During this time, I have been asked by Ron Spagnardi, Bill Miller, and Adam Budofsky to write for the magazine. Last year, David Hakim and David Frangioni approached me to become the Director of Content for the LEGENDS Series. **But this isn't about me!** As of now, there have been a few LEGENDS books that I have directed. Since no "introduction" to any legend should be needed, I wanted to take this opportunity to explain what we are doing with the LEGENDS series.

We devised a new modus operandi that we thought would work very well for LEGENDS. Since each legend had already been interviewed many times for Modern Drummer, had also written books and done instructional videos, and since we were already planning on including all of their previous feature interviews... What use is yet another interview? As one of the LEGENDS team said to me, "How many times can you talk about a drum part to a song, or what kind of sticks do you use?" EXACTLY!

Therefore, we at LEGENDS have done everything to assure that LEGENDS is a *very* different experience. Each book is about all aspects of ONE legendary drummer: New interviews, old interviews, never before seen pictures, transcriptions, artist commentary, and much more. I insisted the new in-depth interviews didn't discuss the same subjects the artists have talked about before in older interviews, especially since those interviews are all included here, side-by-side, in this one book.

As preparation for the LEGENDS interviews, I re-read and take notes on every one of the artists' previous interviews for *Modern Drummer,* I read their books, and I watch their videos. Along the way, I make notes about subjects that I would like to see further expanded upon. I asked the artists if there was anything THEY had never been asked about, or hadn't talked about publicly? Lastly, I research their careers to find any interesting dark corners not yet explored.

For those of you that have been wanting longer interviews, you've come to the right place! There aren't ever any space constraints in LEGENDS. This is where you'll find new 20+ page interviews in the same place as past *Modern Drummer* feature interviews. You'll also find new interviews of these drummers talking about specific sessions and songs throughout their careers, and many pages of them talking about their "gear evolution."

Amazingly, we always come up with a huge list of new and unexplored subjects and questions for every interview. The LEGENDS interviews are not your typical interview. The artist and I take **A LOT** of time to talk. Most importantly, the artists themselves take an integral role in creating this book you are holding. Many legends have contributed rare photos, unheard recordings (included as digital downloads,) their handwritten charts, and other drumming rarities.

The LEGENDS Collection books (in both digital and high quality print formats) are intended to educate and be enjoyed by drummers, other musicians, and music lovers alike. Legendary drumming exists within great music, for me it's always been about music *and* drumming. Many years ago, *Modern Drummer* created the bar for music magazines. In that tradition, we at LEGENDS are raising the bar and setting a new standard for drum and music publications.

– ***Mark Griffith***

A NOTE FROM THE PUBLISHER

Peter Erskine is a true inspiration, one of the most versatile drummers in history, and a musical chameleon! I remember first getting into Peter's playing when he was with Stan Kenton, following him to Maynard Ferguson, and then to one of my all-time favorites, Weather Report. Those three iconic musical settings would be enough for any drummer to establish a career, but over 600 albums later, Peter's musical journey has been, and is, filled with drumming in so many different settings. Quartets, Big Band, Electric Jazz, you name it, and Peter plays it...masterfully!

There is so much to learn from Peter's playing, approach to drums and career that we cannot wait for you to explore this Legends book! You are going to really enjoy reading Peter Erskine Legends, soak it up, go deep into each style and please be as inspired as we were in creating it!

David Frangioni
CEO/Publisher of Modern Drummer Publications, Inc.

Roberto Ciffarelli

Tama Drums

Peter Erskine

The Doctor Is In

By Mark Griffith

Peter Erskine's new band is called Dr. Um. He also has an Honorary Doctorate from Berklee School of Music. But the idea of Dr. Erskine goes much deeper than that. I have never met another drummer who is more tuned into the psychology of being a professional musician than Peter. He will immediately (and humbly) deny this, but it's a fact. I'm sure it helps that his father was a psychiatrist. But it goes even deeper than that. Peter just relates to musical performance on a much deeper level. Prepare yourself for a profound encounter with a true LEGEND! Have a seat on the couch, the doctor will see you now.

"I think from as far back as I can remember, I knew I was going to be a drummer. It wasn't that I *wanted* to be a drummer, I *knew* it. From when I started playing at age 4, I was *going* to be a drummer, that was just it. Period.

My father was a bass player originally, but by the time I was born he was a practicing physician and had become a psychiatrist, but there was always music around the house. He had a conga drum from Cuba, which I still have. As a kid I really enjoyed playing that drum along with some of the recordings he had at home. I actually started taking lessons when I was five. It's funny because as a kid I was the youngest of my family, I had one older brother and two older sisters, and I was spoiled. Whether it was a bottle, food or music, I could just kind of look at something and grunt or point and it would be given to me. My father's doctor friends were worried about the state of my mental development, and they suggested to him that I be tested because I simply grunted a lot. I wasn't speaking because I had everything I needed, and I was very content. The only time that I seemed to really speak up about things, was when it had to do with music. It's odd that this particular acorn seems to have grown into this kind of an oak tree, but it's just always seemed like what I was supposed to do ... it's certainly what I've always enjoyed doing."

> "I think from as far back as I can remember, I knew I was going to be a drummer. It wasn't that I *wanted* to be a drummer, I *knew* it."

Peter might not have talked much as a kid, but as you'll see in this interview, that has changed. He began teaching at the Stan Kenton camps when he joined the band at 18 years of age, and he continues teaching today at USC. Anyone who gets to study drums with him at USC is very lucky. Peter is a master communicator who has built quite a reputation as a master educator. His videos, books, apps, clinics, and play-alongs have invited us along on his journey of drumming and musical discovery. Even a mere visit to his Facebook page isn't met with endless mentions of "my gigs," "my recordings," "me" and "I." It's a learning experience.

MD: I have been following your Infinity Drummers postings and concept on your Facebook page for a while. And for those who don't know what that is, I'll explain. Peter chooses a different drummer every day, and offers a brief thought about, or memory of, that drummer. He also provides a YouTube link to a favorite song that the drummer is on. The drummers are presented in no real order of importance or chronologically. Some of the drummers are well known to us all, and some aren't. I have loved the randomness, and the sincerity of Peter's idea.

Peter: Well thank you! One of the most revealing ways to talk about oneself without actually talking about oneself, is to talk about others. This was a style of discourse that I observed in my first boss, Stan Kenton. He had learned in his later years, that when he was asked to pay tribute to a colleague, he never inserted himself into the conversation. When Stan spoke, it was always just about the other person. I felt that this revealed as much about Stan as it did about the person that he was speaking about. So I always make a conscious effort to do the same.

Whenever someone asks me to make a comment on a drummer that has recently passed, I try to speak without much (if any) use of the pronoun "I" or "me." I was also getting a little tired of saying "Here's something I did" in interviews; So I decided that it would be fun to celebrate some things that someone else did. Most musicians love to play DJ, so those ideas converged as the impetus for the Infinity Drummers idea. Occasionally I do insert myself into the discussion of these drummers, to act as a bridge or to create some relevance.

MD: It also adds some legitimacy or authenticity to your observations when you can draw on some first-hand experiences.

Peter: All of these "Top 10" and "Best of..." lists that people create are highly problematic for me. By focusing on one drummer every day, the Infinity Drummers concept removes the pressure from the creating of my 10 favorite, or the 10 best, or whatever... I didn't have to narrow my point of view, I could just focus on one drummer every day. When the pandemic settled in, and it became obvious that we were going to have plenty of time, I began to consider the contributions of many players, and the Infinity Drummers concept took shape.

The order of the drummers that were chosen was random. The performances that I chose aren't necessarily the best (whatever that means.) Nor were the songs that I linked intended to be the most important or the most popular performances. They're just performances that I have experience with, I have listened to, and that caught my ear. So it's subjective, it's fun, and I'm glad people are enjoying it.

Roberto Ciffarelli

MD: As an extension of that idea, I have picked five very different drummers that I would like you to expound upon. Some of them are lesser known in some circles, which makes it all the more fun. All of them are important to the history of great drumming and music, and I'm guessing pretty important to you, so we'll start there.

I have always heard you as sort of a modern-day Alvin Stoller or Paul Humphrey, so I want to ask you about them. I know you have worked with two bandleaders (Maynard Ferguson and Joe Zawinul) who have played with Frankie Dunlop, and I love Frankie's drumming. Next, you and Steve Gadd both followed in the footsteps of a terrific drummer named Donald MacDonald. Like Steve and yourself, Donald played with Mike Mainieri, and Donald's playing has always knocked me out, unfortunately he's virtually unknown in drum circles. Something tells me that you can shed some light on him for me. And lastly, in my research for this interview I see that you consider the criminally underappreciated Bobby Ramirez to be important to your own development. Those are the five, and those are the reasons that I picked them. But I have a feeling that discussing those guys will lead to many more. Let's start with an early influence of yours, Bobby Ramirez. He was the drummer for the Edgar Winter group called White Trash and later the drummer for the band LaCroix.

Peter: That's quite a list of drummers. I personally didn't know that much about Bobby Ramirez, I knew him through the first two recordings that he made with

Edgar Winter and his band White Trash. The name of the band was funny (maybe ironic) on many levels, because for starters Edgar Winter was an albino and Bobby Ramirez was Mexican-American.

I discovered Bobby Ramirez on those Edgar Winter albums in high school. I was immediately floored by the way this guy played. When I listed him on Infinity Drummers the gratifying and emotionally touching thing was that many of the Facebook comments became a thread of discussion about Bobby. A number of drummers even started talking about how Bobby used to come over to their house, that they knew Bobby, and how they loved his playing as much as I did. Then Willie Ornellas shared some memories about

Cegléd Drum Museum, Peter's first drumset

Courtesy of Cegled Drum Museme

Bobby. They were best friends. Some readers may know Willie because he and Jeff Porcaro were very good friends, and I think Jeff followed Willie into the Sonny and Cher gig. Willie is an excellent drummer unto himself.

Then a musician who worked with a singer that Bobby played with, named Dick Jensen, who I had seen on a clip from the Ed Sullivan show, and who was a big name on the Hawaiian Islands, shared some memories of Bobby. When I saw Dick's name, I googled him, and I saw this incredible performance, and it turns out, it was Bobby Ramirez playing drums. This clip was from before the Edgar Winter band, and the drumming was exciting and dynamic. Bobby Ramirez was kicking this big band on the Ed Sullivan show.

At college, pianist Alan Pasqua, bassist Eric Hochberg, and I would all listen to music together. Alan and I were both really digging those Edgar Winter records, but Eric told us to start listening to Wayne Cochran because he was really hip. So I got a Wayne Cochran record, and the drummer on the record was Allyn Robinson. When I heard the song "Somebody's Been Cuttin' in on my Groove" I felt an instant connection to Allyn's drumming.

Bobby Ramirez' super exciting drumming was kind of the springboard and a connecting of the dots that got me to listening to Allyn Robinson in Wayne Cochran's band. That was very important for me because Jaco Pastorius later joined the Wayne Cochran band, and played along-side of Allyn Robinson. They sounded great together. Those recordings that I heard (before Jaco joined the band, but with Allyn playing,) wound up really influencing my drumbeat. Allyn's influence became a big reason why Jaco had an instant comfort level with my playing, and that's why he wound up recommending me to be the drummer in Weather Report. Jaco could hear Allyn's influence on me by the way that I placed the beat in my R&B playing, and Jaco dug that. There was a familiarity there.

At that time, there was a million great drummers that Jaco could have recommended for that gig. But he recommended me to Wayne Shorter and Joe Zawinul (the leaders of Weather Report.) At the time, Jaco and I had never even played together, think about that. Meanwhile Joe and Wayne were intrigued by me as "the big band guy," because I had played with Stan Kenton and Maynard Ferguson. Personally, I think if Joe or Wayne (who had both played much earlier with Maynard Ferguson) had actually heard me play with Stan or Maynard, they would have given Jaco's suggestion a thumb's down.

Therefore, through listening to music with a couple of musician friends, Bobby's playing led me to Allyn's playing, which affected me enough that Jaco heard a similarity between a drummer that he dug (Allyn Robinson) and myself. And that similarity was so strong that Jaco recommended me for Weather Report. I'll quote (and paraphrase) Hillary Clinton and say that it takes a village of music, musicians, and musical listening to make a musician. Or, as my best friend Jack Fletcher likes to remind me: "The universe is right on schedule." By the way, he is the one responsible for the clever "Dr. Um" title and concept.

"At that time, there were a million great drummers that Jaco could have recommended for that gig. But he recommended me."

MD: I have wanted to ask you about Frankie Dunlop for a while. I love his playing. Everyone is always immediately attracted to his wonderful playing with Thelonious Monk, but he was also an amazing big band drummer. I recently turned some people onto the Maynard Ferguson recording *Message From Birdland* because Frankie's playing is just percolating with excitement. He still had the angularity that he had with Monk, but his time had so much more drive, he was a GREAT big band drummer. That is seemingly forgotten when people remember Frankie's playing. I have always wondered if either Joe Zawinul or Maynard ever mentioned Frankie to you. Because they both played (and recorded) with him; Joe on an early trio recording and Maynard in his big band.

Peter: I'm no authority on Frankie Dunlop's playing, but Joe was in Maynard's band at the same time as Frankie, and I think they got let go from the band at the same time. I love Frankie's playing on "Oleo" from that Birdland recording, like you said, it's just so exciting.

When I first heard that recording, I mistakenly thought it was Rufus "Speedy" Jones. I remember thinking, man Rufus is on FIRE! But it was Frankie Dunlop. You never got the sense that big band drumming wasn't something Frankie was born to do, he isn't *borrowing* the language. As you said, he's a GREAT big band drummer. His snare drum sounds wonderful on that record too.

Interlochen Center for the Arts

Peter's first gig with Stan Kenton, at the Interlochen Summer Arts Camp, 1972

MD: Did you ever hear his later playing with Lionel Hampton's big band?

Peter: See, that's what I mean, musicians love to play DJ!

MD: How about Alvin Stoller? Your more recent playing has reminded me a lot of his playing, and I wondered if there was an influence there?

Peter: After reading an interview with him in **Modern Drummer** years ago, I made a cold call to Alvin to tell him how great his playing was on *West Side Story*. What I didn't know at the time was that half of the drummers in LA either thought they had, or actually did play drums on *West Side Story*. Since then, I have learned that the bulk of the drums that are heard on the original 60's film score of *West Side Story* are actually (probably) Shelly Manne, or at least that's what I believe to be true. But Alvin was doing a lot of the film work at MGM at the time, so who knows. Truthfully, the fact that it could be any of a number of drummers speaks to the level of professionalism that they all had. Those drummers had the professionalism, the versatility, and they could all assume the backing role that the drums had to take on those film soundtracks.

But when I listen to Alvin's playing on (for example) a Frank Sinatra recording, the level of swing is just incredible. I later came to understand drummers like Alvin Stoller or Irv Cottler when I finally did a recording in Studio A at Capitol Recording Studios (which is where many of those Sinatra and Nelson Riddle recordings were made.)

I was recording there with Seth MacFarlane. The drums were in the same room as the rest of the big band, and the strings were in the next room but the wall was open. Therefore, the entire band was essentially in the same space. We did a take, and I did the usual big band drumming thing with setups and such, and we went in to hear the first playback. The first playback on a session is always interesting because you are listening to the sound of your drums, you are listening to how you are interpreting the songs, and you are listening to see if there is anything that you are missing in the arrangements. You are really doing some intense and critical listening for all sorts of stuff. But I had a huge realization when we were listening to the playbacks. I immediately understood why a drummer like Alvin Stoller would play the way that he did. It was because it wasn't only the drum mic's that were picking up the drums. In that type of recording situation, the drums are being picked up by the trumpet mic's, the trombone mic's... The drums are actually leaking into all the mic's in the room.

I came to the realization that if you did this same type of recording with the drums in a booth, there is always a bit of a disconnect, it just doesn't pass the smell test to me. Sorry if that sounds judgmental. When you are in a booth you can always make the decision to play a little harder, a little louder, or just a little more, because the engineer can always just mix the drums down a bit. But when you are in that big room, with all of the other instruments, and the drums are bleeding into all of those mic's, you have to choose your sounds much more carefully.

If you are playing a tune in a large room, or a concert hall, and you are playing a backbeat type of tune, you have to be very aware of what type of sound that you are using. Should you play a cross stick? Should you play the snare drum note in the middle of the drum? Or should you go to a rim shot? Because what many drummers don't realize is that those rimshots gobble up so much frequency range that you wipe out a lot of musical information. If you are playing with a band in a room, you have to remember that the room is the other member of the band. I wish drummers would unlearn the habit of always hitting rimshots.

Alvin Stoller played the way that he did because he really had to tailor his performance so that when he did a "drum thing" it didn't cover up anything else that was happening musically. You have to operate within the musical vocabulary and expectations of the time. When I played that same type of music with Seth, my head couldn't be clouded by "big band drumming" or "fusion" or whatever. And what's really ironic, is that years earlier THAT is exactly why I was hired for the Stan Kenton big band. Because I brought that fusion energy, big band sensibility (or lack of sensibility) to Stan's big band. But as you get older you realize that one approach just doesn't work in all musical contexts, and the older I'm getting, the more I'm being influenced by drummers like Alvin Stoller.

MD: All big bands are not the same, and you have to use your ears, and your musical sensibilities, to serve the music.

"As you get older you realize that one approach just doesn't work in all musical contexts."

Peter: That brings me to the Buddy Rich tribute controversy that I found myself in the middle of years ago. I backed out of the *Burning For Buddy* tribute recordings which created some understandably bad will towards me. In my conversations with Cathy Rich and Steve Arnold, I knew I was on thin ice, but I thought that Buddy's music had to be played on a set that sounded like Buddy's. A 24" bass drum without a pillow, a 13" and 16" tom, no pinstripe heads, and no 10" toms! I thought it would be most effective if everyone played that size set tuned appropriately for the music. If that was done, you would have had everyone essentially playing on the same set, and the playing field would be leveled. That would have really been interesting! As great as a lot of those drumming performances are, both in the live shows and on the recording, it just didn't sound "right" to me. But no one was really interested in that opinion, and so my thoughts fell on deaf ears. Not the first or last time.

It reminds me of the story that Roy Haynes tells about working with Sarah Vaughan when they were splitting a bill with Buddy's band. The story goes that Roy had agreed to play Buddy's kit, and as he sat down, and just barely leaned over to adjust something, Buddy's voice emerged from offstage saying, "Play it as it lays Haynes."

MD: The classic golf phrase.

Peter: When I run live auditions at USC, and drummers come to audition on a school set, I always tell them, no adjusting, just sit down and play. The drums sound fine, it's just like you are sitting in at a jam session.

A while back Larry Klein called me to do a recording session with Eddy Mitchell. I agreed to do it, and then I asked when it was. He replied, "How quick can you get over to Henson Studios? Matt Chamberlain (who was doing the record) has gotten food poisoning, so we'll need you any minute now." I got there as quick as I could, and the band is Leland Sklar, Fred Tackett, Dean Parks, Billy Payne, and some Nashville heavyweights.

So, I walked in and immediately told the engineer that I wasn't going to adjust anything. They had already gotten drum sounds, and these were Matt's drums, so I wouldn't be changing anything. We cut a track and things went well. During the session they asked me if I would want to replace a track that Matt had already recorded the day before, and I told them (in no specific terms) that I had NO interest in replacing anyone's drum tracks. They insisted, so I asked to listen to the track in question. It sounded fine to me, but they really wanted to redo it. I told them that maybe if I added a hi-hat overdub to the existing drum track that it might give them exactly what they were looking for. And it did.

I learned that approach from Jeff Porcaro, he never wanted to replace other drummer's tracks. I always thought of Jeff as the "ethics master" for our generation.

MD: What about Paul Humphrey. I have become enamored with his diversity, and his approach? He can be heard with Steely Dan, Jimmy Smith, Frank Zappa, Marvin Gaye, Jerry Garcia, Etta James, then he took the gig with Lawrence Welk. Has he been an influence on you?

Peter: Like many of the studio musicians of that time, he came to the studio scene with a reputable jazz background. Early on, he played with the Montgomery Brothers, but he became one of the most important R&B drummers in the LA studio scene.

When I was young, I was exposed to a lot of music on TV. The drummers that played on shows like Ed Sullivan and others, always seemed to play on a very professional level. So early on, through TV, the bar was set very high for my drumming, because I wanted to be part of the music that I saw and heard on TV. So much of that music was jazz based because all of the horn players were playing in big bands, and there was so much TV music being made. Every show had an original theme, every station had a little theme, the networks had themes, background music, etc. So without even knowing it, through hearing music on TV, I was hearing drummers like Sol Gubin, Bobby Rosengarden, Grady Tate, and Paul Humphrey.

I learned that TV music was a big part of Jaco's musical lexicon too. Whenever Weather Report sound-checked, unless Joe wanted to rehearse something, we would play music like "The Theme from Goldfinger," or "The Days of Wine and Roses," but I digress.

The first time I heard Paul Humphrey was on the Frank Zappa record *Hot Rats*. That was one of the first times that I heard drums that had that classic dead, single headed, "studio sound." Today that sound is pretty dated and honestly speaking, pretty awful. Paul and John Guerin both had that sound, it was what was popular. But it was a different single headed sound from Hal Blaine. Everyone didn't use that sound, when I listen to Earl Palmer recordings his drums didn't sound like that, Earl's drums always sounded great. Both Paul and John are on a lovely Patrick Williams record called "Carry On," there is two different rhythm section's and they play double drums on an old Johnny Cash song called "The Long Black Veil," that's probably my favorite Paul Humphrey recording. You always knew if you saw his name on a record credit that it was going to be great.

When Paul started playing on the Lawrence Welk show he replaced a drummer named John Klein Jr. who I believe was Lawrence's cousin, he did the show from

"Early on, through TV, the bar was set very high for my drumming, because I wanted to be part of the music that I saw and heard on TV."

1955 to 1976. Paul Humphrey surprised everybody by becoming the drummer on that show. He looked very smart when the musician's union went on strike in 1979. The actors went on strike and the musician's union went on strike in support of the actors. Amazingly, when the musicians later went on strike, the actors didn't support our strike. Because of all of that, every

that he had called. He told me that I should listen to more Lawrence Welk because it was a great place to learn older standard tunes.

Peter: That's one of the best quotes that I have heard in years.

The drumset Yamaha built Peter for Weather Report's final tour of Japan ("final" for that group of players)

Shigeru Uchiyama

musician in LA was having a hard time, no one worked for several months. However, the musicians playing in the *Lawrence Welk Show*, and on the *Tonight Show* were allowed to keep working. I'll bet that Paul took a major amount of criticism from his fellow musicians for doing the Lawrence Welk gig. There were some really good players in that band, I've worked with some of them. But hey, it was a gig, and especially during that strike, I'm sure having that gig was wonderful.

MD: I was playing with (New York pianist) Harold Mabern, and I didn't know a really obscure standard

MD: Have you had any problems throughout your career balancing the studio work, the hip sidemen work, the bandleading work, and the "not so hip" gigs?

Peter: It's been a challenge at times because of different musician's tastes. I was in New York one time, and some younger musicians recognized me and came up to me and asked me why I was doing David Benoit records? And at one time Manfred Eicher (owner and producer of ECM Records) asked me to consider not doing so many recordings outside of the ECM family. Once I had to ask some European musicians to change some scheduling because I was doing a Steely Dan tour, and they got really offended. Everyone has to make choices.

You know Pat Metheny has done it right. And I'll start by saying that I'll never be the musician that Pat is. But Pat, through years of hard road work as a bandleader, created a situation where he only has to appear on recordings that he really wants to. He has been able to craft his amount of output, and I admire that. I never had that luxury.

But the flip side is this: I enjoy the craft of drumming, and if I choose to record the soundtrack to *Cats and Dogs 2: The Adventures of Kitty Galore,* that will inform something in my drumming approach that I can bring to a jazz recording, a hip sideman gig, or as a leader. But a lot of people don't get that.

MD: It's called building a career. I don't care what style of music someone is playing, if they can create a 25-year (or more) career of playing music successfully, they have my deepest respect. No compliments can trump longevity! And as I study your career, I see that.

Peter: You and I are on the same page there. Whenever I meet a drummer or other musician, who has been playing in a band for a long time, I always try to give them the appropriate amount of respect. Whether I like their music or not, there is a certain amount of respect that must be given to longevity in a music career, I agree.

MD: That's why I asked you about Paul, because he seemed to make those same type of career choices. You mentioned that whenever you saw Paul's name on a record you knew it was going to be a good record. And it's strange that you say that, because that's *exactly* the way that I think about you. You have done a lot of good records, and you have done a few great records, but I can't really think of any bad records that I have seen your name on.

Peter: I can! But we won't go there. There is so much to any career that becomes forgotten, for example I had a pretty good jingle career in New York, and no one ever asks me about that. I learned a ton from doing jingles.

MD: That is probably a good way to segue into Donald MacDonald, a drummer that I have always wanted to ask you about, who I believe was pretty busy in the jingle scene too.

Peter: Along with playing with Buddy Rich, and later co-leading Steps and then Steps Ahead, and being a fantastic musician, Mike Mainieri was also a busy jingle producer. He had the unique position of working within the Madison Avenue corporate jingle world, while employing a new generation of musicians on his jingle dates. Mike had a crew of musicians that did a lot of jingle work back in the day in New York City. Mike's musicians were the first generation of musicians to show up to jingle dates not wearing a shirt and tie. These were the days of long hair, tie-dye, buckskin, and fringe. Mike was the bridge between the old school musicians and the new generation of hippie musicians. The first generation of those musicians that I was aware of were guys like Jim Gordon, Gary Burton, Bob Moses, Randy and Michael Brecker, and Jeremy Steig. It was Jeremy who planted the seed of Mike's playing in my head when he mentioned in an interview that his "vibraphonist Mike Mainieri was better than Gary Burton."

Because of Jeremy's boast, I bought Mike's first record called *Insight*, the drummer was Donald MacDonald, and I just totally flipped out over his playing. I love the way that Donald played everything. Looking back, I think I really dug the way that he blended the vertical and the horizontal, and he was a total hippie. His soloing and his comping vocabulary really made an impression on me, and yes he was a major influence on my playing. Then I started to listen to a record by a folk singer named Tim Hardin that I thought that Donald and Mike had done. Years later I found out that it was Earl Palmer and Gary Burton.

MD: I discovered Donald's playing on Mainieri's

"Whenever I meet a drummer or other musician who has been playing for a long time, I always try to give them the appropriate amount of respect."

recording *White Elephant*, which also featured a very young Steve Gadd. Amazingly, I really couldn't tell which tracks were Donald, and which tracks were Gadd. Which (to me) was all that I had to know to know that Donald MacDonald was a fantastic drummer. I went on to buy everything that I could find that he had played on, including *Insight*, which floored me too!

Peter's first percussion overdub, 1972

Peter: He didn't do that many records, but the next one that I picked up was Mainieri's *Journey Through the Electric Tube,* which was pretty wacky. Donald did some Gary McFarland records, along with another great drummer Bill LaVorgna. Then there was a recording of flamenco guitarist Sabicas and Joe Beck called *Sabicas Rock Encounter with Joe Beck*, which had Donald too. Those records represent a time when everything was possible.

At the same time that I was listening to the records that Donald was on, I was also listening to a great deal of Elvin, stylistically and just for that incredible sense of danger, Mel Lewis, Shelly Manne, who was a huge influence, Nick Ceroli was a big influence too. Blakey was one of my bigger influences, Louis Hayes, I was crazy about him. Grady Tate was a phenomenal drummer, Mickey Roker... Of the drummers who have impacted me though, Mel Lewis comes to mind first. I'm thinking of Mel when he was still on the West Coast doing his recordings with Marty Paich, before he went to New York. Mel is just a quintessentially great drummer; he's never made a wrong choice that I've ever found. Then there is the guys today like Ed Soph, John Riley, Bill Stewart, Keith Carlock, Lewis Nash, John Hollenbeck... I'm gonna leave out names, but there are so many players.

A lot of the drummers I like listening to aren't who you'd think. You always hear Tony Williams, Jack DeJohnette, Buddy Rich, if you leave anyone off of that list, it's a sin. Philly Joe Jones, Art Blakey, Roy Haynes... There are so many great drummers. However, I really like listening to a lot of New York drummers like Don

Lamond, Osie Johnson, and Bill LaVorgna, he was a tremendous studio drummer. Donald and Bill LaVorgna were those crossover guys that eventually led me to Bernard Purdie. He changed everything for me.

MD: Speaking of everything changing, I thought that I heard a very specific change in your playing about 20 years ago. Maybe it was because of the ECM trio recordings, and the influence of that sound. But I heard a very specific Paul Motian influence in your playing that I hadn't heard previously, and I wondered if that is an accurate observation, and where that came from?

Peter: The iconic recordings that he did with Bill Evans and Scott LaFaro at the Village Vanguard stood out to me for the stark nobility of Motian's drumming. I was also a big fan of his drumming with Keith Jarrett on *Expectations* as well. I didn't start listening to Keith's American quartet (with Motian and Charlie Haden and Dewey Redman) until much later.

I play *Expectations* for students a lot, and I played it for one very bright student, and he made the astute observation that, "Paul Motian is letting the music do all of the work." That got him an A+ for life! I asked Motian about his time with Bill Evans once and he said simply, "It was a good gig." When I asked him to elaborate, he said sort of flippantly, "I'm writing my own book."

MD: That could be taken many ways.

Peter at age 14 rehearsing with Dave Brubeck

Interlochen Center for the Arts

Peter: That's the way Paul played, he was indeed writing his own book. I saw his trio with Joe Lovano and Bill Frisell once and it was (and I'm not trying to be clever) a study in motion. The stark orchestration, the stark amount of notes, it was so unique. The way that Motian moved when he hit a cymbal or a drum was so refreshingly free of any sort of preparation stroke.

That preparation stroke has always been a bit of a curse for me. The guy that pointed this out to me was Vic Firth. I was doing a tympani overdub on a Doc

Severinsen album years ago, and the arranger told me that my entrance was late on several takes, so we redid them. On the next take I purposely jumped the gun, and he said it was fine. I remember wondering, "What was that about?" I explained the situation to Vic Firth at the next PAS Convention, and he asked me to show him what I did. As soon as I began to play a note (with my big preparation stroke) he stops me and says, "What's all this?" And he moves his arms in a big windup, no wonder you were late. That will throw your time off." The dots connected for me, and I remembered that Zawinul and Wayne were trying to tell me about that many years earlier, but they didn't know how to put it into drum terms. But (I think) that's what they meant, my preparation stroke was delaying my time feel.

If you watch drummers like Alex Acuña, Levon Helm, or Paul Motian there is a beautiful directness to their stroke that lacks that upstroke. The directness of their stroke always seems to make their time just a little bit better than most. I would suspect that Keltner probably has it too.

MD: I did find that you referenced Motian in one older interview, where you said, "The more that I learn about Jeff Porcaro the more that I understand Paul Motian." What an interesting thought, and I have to ask you about that.

Peter: That is interesting, I don't remember saying that. But I probably was saying to play what's important and play it in the right place. I'm no authority on Jeff either, and if we started talking about him I would probably start asking you more questions than giving you answers. When Jeff played, he didn't mess around, there was a wonderful directness to his playing.

Listening to Jeff also taught me about the space between the notes. I was in Tower Records in Osaka Japan, they were playing a Toto record and I was listening to his pocket, I was listening and marveling at his backbeat. Then my ear was drawn to the rhythm guitar, and the synergy between the drums and the guitar. And that was it! It was the deep hook-up between the drums and the guitar.

MD: You use the word intent a lot. I think Jeff played with a great amount of intent.

Peter: I was doing a short Boz Scaggs tour back in 1994, and Lenny Castro was playing percussion. And I guess that I was doing a pretty good "Jeff imitation." But one night I made a specific drumming choice that wasn't something that Jeff had actually played. I immediately felt Lenny's stare, then he smiled and yelled out to me, "Now you get it!" I would be at a loss to explain exactly what I did in that moment, but Lenny felt it, and so did I. It's something that you can't describe, transcribe, or bottle. Sure, it's intention, but I also think it's just honesty.

The other side of honesty happened to me when I toured with Steely Dan. We were rehearsing "Reelin' in the Years," and I dislike the song so much that I'm sure it felt just awful. To make things worse, Donald Fagen had come up with an arrangement that sounded like the Doobie Brothers meets Shaft. I'm totally not buying the arrangement, and I'm just dutifully doing my job playing this tune that I really don't like. I don't recommend this, but I decided to completely turn down my in-ear monitors. Then I started singing imaginary Count Basie style background choruses to myself along with the song (since it's a shuffle.) Then Walter Becker comes up to the drums and gives me a big thumbs up. Why did that happen? Because I was playing the truth, I was being honest.

"The way that Paul Motian moved when he hit a cymbal or a drum was so refreshingly free of any sort of preparation stroke."

MD: Both Motian and Porcaro had that honesty and directness in their playing. Maybe that's what you are getting at. In a past Legends interview with Chad Smith, he said something very interesting to me. He said that maybe the evolution of starting as a young musician who plays hard and takes up as much space as possible, to becoming an older musician who lets the drums speak a little more and sees the beauty of leaving space, has to happen in that order. Meaning that it's just human nature to evolve that way. You have actually evolved that way as well. In the Weather Report days, you played hard and very densely. Now you are letting the drums speak more and leaving a little more space. Can you comment on that evolution in your own playing?

Peter: I think Chad was making a very good point there. When you are young you have posters of scantily clad women, and fast flashy sports cars, so it's natural to play like that.

But I was a slightly different kind of kid. In high school I had posters of Sigmund Freud, Martin Luther King Jr., and, okay, Jane Fonda. In college I had posters of Issac Hayes, Frank Zappa and John Coltrane.

When I got the *Rich vs. Roach* record at six, I identified much more with Max than I did Buddy. As great as Buddy was, I couldn't identify so much with him. The technique intimidated me. But when it came time for Max's solo, the bass is walking, and Max is playing the music like he's a saxophone player, it was so utterly melodic. I was quite young, but I immediately recognized that I could relate to that.

My first teacher talked more about Sol Gubin and Art Blakey than Buddy Rich, and he didn't stress the rudiments much at all. I actually had a traumatic experience as a kid when a later drum teacher made fun of me for not knowing my rudiments. I started crying, because the guy made fun of my old drum teacher for not teaching me the rudiments.

Speaking of tears, there are only two drummers that have ever made me cry. One was Elvin playing "Vigil" with John Coltrane, and the other was Jeff Porcaro playing "That's Why" with Michael McDonald. Both made me weep because they were the first times that I had identified something as THE perfect drum track. It was like seeing Michelangelo's *Pieta* for the first time. I just didn't know music or drumming could be *that perfect*. That was also when I realized that I would *never* be able to do *that*. Part of me died when I realized that. But it was a necessary death, because that was the only way that I could continue to grow as a drummer.

"There are only two drummers that have ever made me cry. One was Elvin playing "Vigil" with John Coltrane, and the other was Jeff Porcaro playing "That's Why" with Michael McDonald."

As I think back to those days, when I was in my late 20's, it was a rough time. I was in New York struggling to make it, I was struggling with the instrument, and I was wrestling with ego. I listen back to some of the stuff that I played, and I cringe, I read some of the stuff I said and it's embarrassing. I'm still working on the concept of forgiving myself.

One of the greatest lessons I've learned was a gift from a producer who called me up after one of my first recording sessions in New York. He said, "I just wanted to tell you that your bullshit jazz attitude was a complete drag last night, and no one appreciated it." I was shocked because I felt I had played well, but I spent a lot of time thinking about it. I have to admit that he was right, I was trying to be a smart aleck and talking too much. But realizing that you have to say goodbye to parts of yourself, or just realizing what a complete idiot you are, is all part of growing up as a person, and as a musician.

MD: I think that's part of what Chad was getting to as well.

Peter: When you're young you play for yourself and you're trying to figure out how to play, you're wrestling with the instrument, your ego, and your identity. As you get older you realize it's more about playing what you would like to hear, not what you want to play. I always just try to imagine I'm listening to the music. That makes it very easy for me to make a musical choice. If you have no idea what you want to hear, now *that's* an issue. But if you're informed enough musically then you can trust your instincts. You're just playing what you'd like to hear. That means that you're a hundred percent involved with the music as it's being played. If you're not a hundred percent involved, then your mind is on something else and that's not in the service or to the benefit of the music, you're just playing for your ego.

MD: I am fascinated by how people relate to, and develop their touch on the drums, and I have always admired your touch. At Indiana University you studied with George Gaber, he intrigues me. How did Gaber approach teaching "touch" to you?

Peter: He would demonstrate touch by playing timpani. George Gaber was into allowing self-discovery. He believed that was pivotal for the student. His lessons about "touch" started for me one day in the middle of a lesson. George suddenly picked up a triangle, and said, "OK, mezzo-piano you get one chance." I played (what I thought to be) a single strike at mezzo-piano, and he said, "Too loud, now get out." I went home, I didn't have a triangle, but a cymbal was the next best thing, so I started playing long tones (whole notes) on a ride cymbal. That started a lifelong fascination with playing long tones on a cymbal. When you play a beat, it's the tone that determines how it feels. It's your touch that determines the tone. When I think back on any recording that I have done, that I don't like, it's my touch and my tone that has created what I didn't like.

There was a guitarist playing with Joe Zawinul once, and he recorded a solo on a take that Joe planned on using. When the guitarist found out that Joe was going to use that take for the record, the guitarist requested that he be allowed to re-record his solo, because he didn't like what he had played. Joe turned to him and said, "If you didn't like what you played… Then why did you play it?"

During Jaco's Word of Mouth tour of Japan

Shigeru Uchiyama

If you have control over your touch, you can take ownership of your sound and your tone, then you can take ownership in what you are playing. But it all starts with your touch. When I took lessons with Freddie Gruber he demonstrated "touch" as a tap dancer dancing on top of the floor, not stomping through the floor. That resonated back to what Gaber was saying, and even to what Wayne and Joe were trying to tell me. When you watch Papa Jo or Philly Joe play, that's what you are watching. They are drawing the sound out of the instrument, not playing into it. "Touch" for me, has to do with volume control, and the quality of the sound. For me, it starts with the stroke, and how you are holding the stick. Is the stick vibrating in your hands or is it choked? Teaching good touch is to encourage good tone production. But ultimately, I think the student has to experience it and work on it for themselves.

I learned a big lesson from trumpet player Wayne Bergeron. Whenever he's done with a gig, he always warms *down*. It's that dedication and attention to your own body-instrument that I aspire to. When I warm up it's all about tone and consistency. It's not about speed or whatever. It's a communion with the room, the surface that I'm playing, the sticks, and my body. I'm saying hello to all of those things. Everything else will follow.

MD: Taking ownership of one's playing seems to go directly against the modern digital technology of fixing any mistake or blemish that might exist in a song or a track. Talk to me about the importance of making mistakes.

Peter: Like you said, digital technology has made the erasure or the spot fixing of (almost) anything quite easy. But the ability to record something "old school" requires a different level of commitment to the performance.

I'll offer some very practical modern drum recording advice. Now if you are Jim Keltner, Steve Gadd, Jeff Porcaro, Allan Schwartzberg, Chris Parker, or Jim Gordon you never have to do this. Those guys put the pocket in the perfect place every single time. This trick is unnecessary for them. But for us mere mortals working

today… If you ever lay down a track, and any part of it feels a little on top of the beat, go into pro-tools and select all of the drum tracks, and move them to the right (back) by ten milliseconds, add the crossfades, and you will be astonished. Instantly the track will feel much better. I'm not embarrassed to admit that I have used this trick a few times in recent years.

I remember Pat Metheny saying that a track or a solo can always be better. I get that. But my reply was that it can never be the same as when you commit to a live-to-two-track recording, and that's the only shot that you get. There is a palpable difference. My favorite jazz records were the ones that were made in one or two afternoons and there were mistakes.

The Dr. Um Band from left: John Beasley, Bob Sheppard (sax) Benjamin Shepherd and Peter, at a show in Chicago.

Peter Erskine Library

On my record *Sweet Soul*, there is a track called "Touch Her Soft Lips and Part" and Joe Lovano, Marc Johnson, and Kenny Werner all played so heartbreakingly beautiful it's just breathtaking. But there is a spot where pianist Kenny Werner plays one of those one finger on two keys "mistakes." My dad heard the record and asked, "Can't you fix that?" I told him that THAT was possibly my favorite moment on the whole record. I loved the humanity of it.

MD: When I interviewed Steve Smith, he recalled taking lessons with you at a Stan Kenton camp. He remembered that you had a fantastic way of explaining time. In a video much later, you talked about thinking of different subdivisions (sixteenths or triplets) between a note and how that affeced the feeling of the time; even if you weren't actually playing the subdivisions. Is that what you were talking about in the Kenton camps?

Peter: For me it is about being able to play consistent quarter notes and creating a ride cymbal pattern that works for the band. All the while being able to stay consistent with the ride cymbal while you are doing all of the other (fun) stuff. I think that's what Steve is remembering. I find that if I cheat the space between the notes, it just never feels right.

Russ Miller and I were trading lessons a while back. He wanted to ask me about playing the jazz ride cymbal pattern. And for my lesson with him, I asked him a very simple question. "Why are people calling *you* for gigs? What makes *you* so special?" It might look condescending in print, but that's **not** how I meant it. He said that the only thing that he could think of was that he played long backbeats. I asked him what he meant by that, and he explained further. "When most drummers play backbeat music, they think of it as boom, bap, boom, bap… I think of it as boom, baaaah, boom, baaaah." My world instantly went from gray to technicolor!

MD: Is that what you refer to as legato drumming?

Peter: No. Legato drumming is melodic drumming. It is the ability to render any series of rhythms in the same way that a horn player does. Max Roach and Joe Morello came up with this when they started to play melodies on the drum set. It's being aware of note length, and the shape of the note. Singing what you play is the introduction to legato drumming (or playing in general.) I have bass students at USC too, and I teach it to them as well. Ron Carter once asked me sarcastically, "What does a drummer teach a bass student?" I told him that I tell them to listen to a lot more (bassist) George Duvivier. He was a master of shaping the notes of a bassine. Ron smiled and gave me a hug.

One of my most recent teaching methods is this. I like to think that we all have these imaginary whirling discs of time rotating in our minds. And they all have different subdivisions on them. One disc spins and creates quarter notes, one creates the sound of whole notes, etc… But they are all whirling at the same time in a sort of vertical plane.

MD: Like a stack of spinning dishes?

Peter: Yes. And we can pull one of those pulses from any of those vertical whirling discs into our playing at any time. But then students ask how can they be aware of all of them at all times? Which brings me to my second "new" point.

If you are doing a simple task like driving to the store, you are thinking of many things at the same time. You get in the car. Do I have enough gas? Put the car in reverse, make sure not to back over your neighbor who is walking her dog! Shift into drive, don't speed! Put on your blinker, make a left here to avoid traffic. What do I need from the store again? Bread, but don't forget the milk…. In a simple trip to the store, we are thinking of dozens of things at the same time. So, if you can handle that, you can handle the rhythmic awareness of thinking of many different rhythmic subdivisions, a long backbeat, and dynamics, all at the same time. Who says that we can't we think of several subdivisions at the same time?

MD: Especially if they are all related.

Peter: So much of this comes from the bassist that I played with in the Kenton band. His name was John Worster. He really started me thinking about feeling the subdivisions between the quarter notes. The Kenton band played some very slow tunes, so I had to really get my time together. These lessons came full circle recently when I was in the recording studio on the first day of recording the Joni Mitchell with Symphony Orchestra project called *Both Sides Now*.

I'm playing brushes in this large orchestra (and orchestras tend to be a little sluggish.) We were at the beginning of the project, and we weren't using a click track, so I'm trying to push the orchestra along. When I listened to the playback of this first take, the drums sounded like a bull in a china shop. It just was too heavy. I had to figure out how to provide rhythmic information without playing the obvious set-ups. I wanted everyone to feel where the beat was, I didn't want to step on any of Joni's vocals, and I didn't want to sound too muscular, these were love songs that we were playing.

I was able to figure out pretty quickly how I could provide just enough rhythmic hints and to trust that if I played a good, steady, but quiet, and insistent beat, that would work a lot better than trying to overplay the situation.

MD: That is the art of accompaniment.

Peter: There's a lot of power in a whisper, so that's just a little bit of an operating principle for me (at the drums of all places.) For me the music works better when you don't push it too hard, when you don't try too hard, and when you leave a little bit of space.

For all this over-analyzing that I sometimes do, it's nice to leave the other musicians and the listeners with a question. I don't think music should provide all the answers. I think it should provoke some questions. For a while it seemed like (especially with fusion) BOOM we're going to answer everything and here it ALL is. A note wouldn't be left un-played, and no questions were left un-answered. I was as guilty of that as anybody. Recently, I've found myself drawn more to musical settings or a musical approach that takes shadow and space into account. It just seems like more interesting things happen when I do that.

Any dissatisfaction I have ever had with my drumming, (which can be a lot,) usually has had to do with if I feel that I'm muscling the music. I really don't like muscling the music. Like I said, if you want the one shortest, simplest and maybe the best drum lesson that I could possibly give, here it is: Just play what you want to hear, play what you'd like to hear. I tell my college students that all four years of study can be shaved

"Recently, I've found myself drawn more to musical settings or a musical approach that takes shadow and space into account."

down to just that.

MD: You have mentioned a few times that Zawinul and Wayne Shorter were giving you advice and direction on your drumming when you were in Weather Report. I've heard that you had some infamous "drum lessons" with Zawinul during soundchecks in the Weather Report days.

Playing with the Kenton band

Erskine Library

Peter: I always listened to Joe, sometimes even to Jaco's consternation. Joe set very high standards with his improvisational ideal of "We always solo, we never solo." That was an ideal that was hard for most mortals to reach. He also came from the old school, school of hard knocks, macho, what doesn't kill me makes me stronger, attitude. You had to be able to take the heat in the kitchen (so to speak).

Joe often didn't know how to explain what he wanted, and I didn't know how to understand what he wanted. Many times, he would wind up showing me different beats. Yet every beat that he would play was this same boogie-woogie kind of beat. I would tell him that the song that we were talking about is a totally different feel and tempo. I didn't realize until much later, probably after I had left the band, that he was just trying to show me how he wanted the groove and the music to "dance." Because of this, I often tell students that sometimes musicians have a hard time finding the right words to describe what they want.

MD: That's another type of listening that's important.

Peter: Near the end of my stay in Weather Report, we were touring with a big lighting and sound rig. The heat would get really oppressive on stage, because in some venues this lighting rig hung very low. The last tune that we would play on that tour was a really fast double time swing type of thing. I asked Joe if it would be alright if I signaled him for the last time through. I just didn't want to run out of steam, I wanted to end the night on a high note. That seems like a reasonable request, right?

So that night, I gave him the signal, and he lowered

his head below his top keyboard as if he didn't see me. Then his volume increased, and we had to go through the form of the tune again. We, as a band, had missed the exit ramp. I felt betrayed and angry. I started hitting the drums even harder in my fury, and we come to the ending again. Joe signals the end, the lighting guy gets the cue, and I (purposely) don't stop.

There was a whole choreographed ending to the show, but I was so mad that I just kept playing. The lighting guy caught the situation and put a spotlight on me. I was playing as hard as I could, and with a frenzy that I had never felt. I listened to myself a bit and noticed that I was sounding a little like Eric Gravatt. It had that much energy! But I couldn't figure out how to end it. My eyes were closed, I'm playing, and I sensed a presence. Zawinul had climbed up onto the edge of the drum riser, and he was standing right in front of my bass drum. For a moment, I thought that he was going to punch me. Instead, he had this look of complete ecstasy, he starts yelling "Yeah! Yeah! Yeah…" And he jumps off the riser, pumps his fist in the air, which I caught on the drums, and when he landed, I hit a big crash and ended the show.

I saw him briefly backstage, and he says, "Thank You." I replied, *"Thank you for what?"* The next day at soundcheck, the road manager says, 'Peter, Joe would like to talk to you." I thought, this is it, I'm going to get fired. And I walk into the dressing room and there is Zawinul with the entire band and crew. And everyone is holding little dixie cups filled with cognac. Joe hands me a cup, and he raises his drink and says, "Everyone, last night, Peter graduated." I didn't get fired, as it turns out Joe had been waiting for me to finally assert myself musically. I had been a sideman for so long, and I didn't feel that I had enough command or control of the instrument to assert myself. That wouldn't come for many years.

MD: So how can you tell when you have, or are ready to "graduate" if you aren't lucky enough to have a Joe Zawinul to tell you so?

Peter: Interesting. I don't think most bands require a "graduation day." I think most bandleaders are assuming that you have already graduated. When I did the audition with Weather Report, they were all really late to the "audition-rehearsal." When they finally arrived, I just sat down and started playing. I didn't play the happy sideman then either.

MD: Maybe that's why you got the gig. You were pissed off. And then you finally "graduated" when they pissed you off again. I'm seeing a pattern here.

Peter: But this also goes back to the Boz Scaggs-Lenny Castro story. That was a graduation of sorts too. By that time, I had acclimated, and studied Boz's music enough that I wasn't just imitating what Jeff had played, I had reached a level where, as Lenny said, "Now you understand *why* Jeff played what he played." I felt like he meant that I was approaching the music on the music's own terms. And this is not to imply that I think that my pocket or feel is anywhere remotely close to Jeff's! But that's easier to do when you're an older person than when you are a "young buck." When you are older, expectations and musical motivations are quite different from when you're young.

"When you are older, expectations and musical motivations are quite different from when you're young."

MD: And that's what made Jeff so special. He played that way when he was really young. Some people say he was born an "old soul." We are talking about psychology here, not music. But it's all really the same thing.

I can't help but think that you are so aware of this aspect of playing music because your father was a psychiatrist. So I'll ask this question with all the "young bucks," (who think that they have all of this stuff already figured out,) in mind. When did all of this start to make sense to you? And when did you first realize that you were beginning to figure this stuff out.

Peter: I'm not really there yet, but I think I'm getting close. I benefitted from the generosity and advice of so many of the drum elders. Some of them would "give it up," but many of them wouldn't. And by "it" I mean direct advice. Some of them would show their generosity and advice by playing the role of "gate keeper," or by telling you that you didn't have the "right keys yet." Whereas others would give it up and tell you that you were ready to be part of the club, *even if you weren't*. The ecosystem of drumming is generally one of support for one another.

MD: Back to your dad's career as a psychiatrist, do you think that has helped you get as close as you are to figuring out music-psychology, or the psychology of playing music.

Peter: Completely. Absolutely. My dad was a man of science, and he enjoyed teaching. By the time I was born, my dad had become a psychiatrist and he had a lot of time for me. We were buddies. I asked him EVERYTHING! He really taught me that there was no such thing as a stupid question, and he fueled my constant curiosity.

But before he became a doctor he was a musician, a bass player. He always told me that I wasn't digging into the ride cymbal enough. He also told me to always "give something" to someone before you attempt "to take something away."

MD: That is great life advice.

Peter: I've used that bit of advice a lot. Another thing to realize is that at one time or another everyone has "impostor syndrome." Everyone wonders (at times) if they are really "up to snuff." I believe that most of us are really just trying to do our best.

But there were MANY times that I used very poor psychology as well. I made a lot of mistakes in work situations. If I acquired any smarts at all, it is because I made so many dopey mistakes.

MD: But even with that admission, you show a great deal of wisdom. Part of being a magnificent teacher (I think) is talking about and sharing your mistakes. How has the pandemic affected your own business model, and career?

Peter: Entrepreneurially, thankfully my business model has been expanding over time. Many years ago, (after seeing my daily and monthly schedule) Bob Beals (of

CBS 30th Street Studio, during recording of "Airegin" for Maynard Ferguson (New Vintage album)

Gordon Johnson

Evans drumheads) told me that I needed to find a way to make money while I was asleep. That is what got me thinking about royalties. His comment prompted me to try and take a little more control over my creative and financial destiny.

I have been involved in signature drum products for a while, I have a small studio here at home, I compose music for theater, and I have been writing books, recording videos, and creating apps for quite a while. Unfortunately, I realize that I might not have promoted those endeavors as well as I could. I was always moving on to the next thing. I have been guilty of trying to wear too many hats, and so I would warn people against that. I'm not a very good marketer, I am very bad at completing the circle from production to distribution to promotion. By the time I get to the promotion phase I see a new "thing" and I start to chase that. I'm trying to pay more attention to that stuff now. Like I said, I've made mistakes.

Most recently I have learned the mantra-saying, *"What's stopping you?"* I like that way of thinking and I am trying to adopt that into my life. The role model for the subject of business is Vic Firth. He was an incredible artist, a visionary in the musical instrument industry, and an icon. He started out making tympani mallets in his house, became an integral part of the Percussive Arts Society. He was a dashing figure in both the drum and percussion worlds, and he began as a drum set player. Bassist Buell Neidlinger told me once what made Vic so special as a tympanist; It was his pitch. He told me that the whole Boston Symphony Orchestra was built upon Vic's amazing sense of pitch and tone.

Through my last 20 years of teaching at USC, I am very proud of the fact that I have found a balance between teaching and performing. My students can hear me on records and doing gigs, which I think is important. And I enjoy being a bandleader of a few different ensembles. I am really proud of how all of the play-along apps (that I have developed with Lucas Ives) have been used by other teachers. They have been well accepted and some teachers are using them very creatively. Our app engine supports full mixing capabilities, and we are releasing new recordings in that play along format.

MD: How about how the pandemic has affected you creatively?

Peter: I just did my first gig since this whole thing began. It was with the Lounge Art Ensemble, which is a saxophone trio, and the crowd was small and vaccinated. When we were playing as an ensemble, if felt great, but for trading or soloing I felt that anything that I played didn't have much substance to it. I have talked to a few other musicians about this and found out that I am not alone in this feeling. It seems that the bicycle is not quite as rideable (as we might think) when you have been off of it for so long. Maybe we have been musically and artistically traumatized more than we realized by this whole situation. Not that the artistic trauma compares in any way to the human tragedy and the loss of lives that has occurred and is occurring.

MD: That's not surprising to me because playing music is not only interacting with the other musicians, but it is interacting with oneself, and interacting with the music in real time; Not to mention how the musicians and the music interact with the listeners. And unfortunately, that interaction has been changing and lessening in how we create and how we listen to music for quite a while, long before the pandemic.

Peter: My label (Fuzzy Music) was originally a way to declare and define artistic independence. But we just pulled the plug on our label producing physical recordings, it's been gratifying, and I think we made some very good records, but my wife and I just got exhausted from banging our heads against the wall. Today, everyone wants their music for free, which is a problem.

It turns out that maybe the musical gatekeepers (A&R people, label heads, and producers) were a good thing. Now that everyone has a studio in their garage and can release music whenever and however they want... people just *expect* it to be free. It's seems like maybe the democratization of the music business isn't really working out that well.

The labels and the major studios used to create very high quality and incredible music productions. There were these amazing music scenes not only in LA and New York, but in Nashville, Dallas, Chicago, Memphis, Detroit, Philadelphia, not to mention internationally. But now people don't want to pay for music. And I can

"Most recently I have learned the mantra-saying, 'What's stopping you?' I like that way of thinking and I am trying to adopt that into my life."

tell you first-hand that the miniscule financial rewards from streaming on whatever platform don't justify 10 or 20 or 30 thousand dollars to invest into creating a recording.

MD: Arrangers, producers, engineers, good studios, and good musicians cost money.

Peter: Because of this, it just seems to me that the quality of the music that is being released today has suffered. I have a hard time finding new and inspiring recordings. The playing ability for musicians today has never been higher. I see the drummers on YouTube, and some of them make some very nice productions. But…

MD: How are they making any money? The fact is that it takes money to survive in today's world. And releasing videos and music on YouTube isn't providing nearly enough income for anyone to live or even survive. And it's not just musicians. It's writers, photographers, actors, and the support staff that goes into all of that.

Peter: Here (you and I) are speaking as cultural gatekeepers or at least cultural liaisons, and the paradigm has shifted for this next generation of musicians. There has to be a bit of a reckoning because for the first time in my life, I have a hard time imagining how all of the information that I am teaching, and talking about here with you, is going to be used by the readers, our students, or the musicians of the next generation. The structure of everything creative seems that it has been thrown to the ground and broken. Maybe there will be a cultural renaissance, and I just don't have the crystal ball to know what it will be, I hope so!

MD: I hope that this entire COVID pandemic and the year-long quarantine, will kickstart a cultural renaissance. I hope it makes people starved for cultural interaction and face to face (same time and place) communication.

Sure, there will be some changes, I think Zoom and video conferencing will (and has) become much more accepted and is here to stay. But even through that we have lost the idea of *time* and *place*. Sure, you and I are talking at the same *time*, but what *place* are we speaking in? Because *that place* determines *what* and *how* we say things. I think the modern conundrum of *time and place* will also eventually affect the new idea of working from home as well.

The place where we create and listen to music, and how we obtain the music, determines the relationship between the music, musicians, and the listeners. That interaction is really what music and culture is.

Peter: You have to promise me that you will print everything that you just said. You said it perfectly!

MD: Lastly, can I ask you about the recording we included as a digital download of you playing a solo when you were nine-years-old with the Stan Kenton band? You sounded really good as a kid!

Peter: That is Max Roach by way of Joe Morello. The solo wasn't planned, I was sitting in with the Kenton band in 1963, and Stan says, "Play something Peter!" So I start to solo, and the piano and bass start to play a vamp. That's still my favorite way to solo. My vocabulary is quite melodic, and compositionally the solo is pretty sound. Amazingly, I joined the Kenton band nine years later.

I find it fascinating that I can go back almost 60 years, and hear the same qualities in my drumming then, as I can today, for better or worse. That's why I began the interview by saying it just always seemed like this is what I was supposed to do, it's certainly what I've always enjoyed doing.

I read a book called *We've Had 100 Years of Psychotherapy and the World is Getting Worse* by James Hillman and Michael Ventura. In it, they mention a bullfighter, and the folklore surrounding him was that as a boy he used to hide behind his mother's skirt, just as a bullfighter uses a piece of fabric to hide behind and trick the bull. The authors postulate that somewhere in that young boy, he knew his own destiny. And that he knew that someday he would be fighting bulls, hiding behind, and equipped only, with a piece of fabric as protection.

Some people are lucky enough that their destiny reveals itself, and they know what they are going to become. For me, that's what this solo with Kenton as a nine-year old boy represents. I knew that I wanted to become a drummer that was a mixture of Max Roach, Joe Morello, Art Blakey, Shelly Manne, Mel Lewis, Grady Tate, Don Lamond, and Elvin Jones. So today with the Infinity Drummers, and everything that I do, I'm still that same nine-year-old drummer, and I'm still continuing that marvelous experience of learning.

MD: And playing, and teaching!

THE DOWNLOADS

FUZZY MEMORY MUSIC ARCHIVES

Thanks to Peter's record label Fuzzy Music, we are proud to include several free downloads of Peter Erskine's most compelling work. You'll find your download code on the title page of this Legends book.

The first download is the earliest known recording of Peter Erskine. There are no pots and pans here, and this is no vanity recording. It's a recording of nine-year-old Peter playing a solo with the great Stan Kenton. This recording has already been included in Peter's *Drum Perspectives* book on Alfred Music, but it's good enough to include again. The recording, and Peter's insightful commentary (below,) provide some interesting insight into the musician, and the man. Peter's transcription (on the following page) shows Peter's early understanding of jazz drumming, creativity, and touch.

The next three downloads, (dating from 1997, 2001, and 2016,) offer three (very different) tracks from Peter's own recordings that are all transcribed here in Legends. "Cats and Kittens," "Boogie Shuttle Stop," and "Hawaii Bathing Suit" are highlights from three of Peter's bands: Lounge Art Ensemble, The Trio with Alan Pasqua and Dave Carpenter, and Dr. Um.

The last download is a never-before-heard alternate take of another tune that Legends has transcribed, called "Furs on Ice." This was an exciting song performed live on tour by John Abercrombie, Marc Johnson, and Peter Erskine. Thankfully, Peter had his DAT recorder on for the whole tour, and we can now hear another interpretation of this wonderful song.

Peter Erskine Library

***Drum solo with Stan Kenton (from Drum Perspectives book,) featuring nine-year-old Peter Erskine* playing a drum solo.**

Peter recalls the circumstances regarding this solo with joy and pride, "Summer 1963: Bloomington, Indiana. My parents drove me all the way from Linwood, New Jersey to Indiana so I could attend the Stan Kenton National Stage Band Camp. At the final concert of the camp, I played a song (and this solo) with the Stan Kenton Orchestra. Exactly nine years later I would be Stan's drummer! The solo at the end of the song was an impromptu moment, and if you listen carefully, you can hear Stan telling me, "Play Peter!"

The Joe Morello solo on Dave Brubeck's recording of "Take Five" is an obvious influence here. What's interesting is that no matter what else I've learned over the years, I still essentially play and sound quite the same as I did when I was a child. This is further fuel for the *acorn growing into a tree argument*, (i.e. we are who and what we are.) At least it's nice to think that way about the better qualities of our being. Pardon the indulgence, but I thought the inclusion of this solo would be entertaining if not instructive."

"Peter at Age Nine" solo

V = press stick into head resulting in a pitch bend.

"Cats and Kittens," *Lounge Art Ensemble, Lava Jazz.*

Saxophone trios (saxophone, bass, and drums) are a very exciting musical instrumentation with a rich musical history. Harmonically, the instrumentation affords more flexibility and freedom to the bassist and saxophonist. For drummers, the absence of a chordal instrument creates more space to interact and more opportunity to direct and shape the music. On "Cats and Kittens" Peter's rollicking groove does just that, and the Lounge Art Ensemble takes its place in the rich history of the saxophone trio.

"Boogie Shuttle Stop," Alan Pasqua, Dave Carpenter, Peter Erskine, *Badlands.*

The musical relationship between Peter Erskine, pianist Alan Pasqua, and the late bassist Dave Carpenter was magical. They were a trio that had one foot in the past and one foot in the future. The Trio was swinging, impressionistic, unbridled, and fun. The (included) transcription shows all of this and more. Written by bassist Dave Carpenter, we wanted to include "Boogie Shuttle Stop" as a tribute to the great bassist, and Peter's good friend, Dave Carpenter.

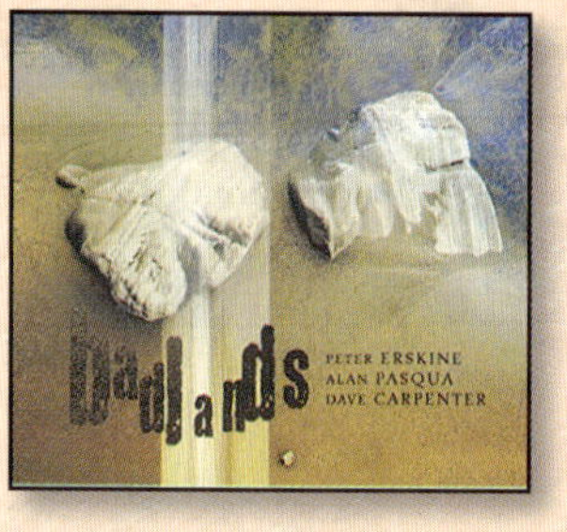

"Hawaii Bathing Suit," Peter Erskine, *Dr. Um.*

With his new band ,called Dr. Um, Peter seems to have accepted his Weather Report past. While the comparison of the two bands is rather easy, (due to the same instrumentation,) Dr. Um is much more than that. Today, Dr. Um's collective groove creates the same type of "dance," that Joe Zawinul was trying to coax out of Peter years ago. Today The Weather Report comparisons are strengthened further by the touring Dr. Um band including John Beasley's creative synth work, Benjamin Shepherd's slinky bass playing, and Bob Sheppard's playful saxophone, not to mention the joyous attitude of Erskine's composition. This is a band to be reckoned with. It's hard to believe that this song was turned down for so many projects. Maybe the song just had to find the right band, and it did.

"Furs on Ice," (alternate take,) *Abercrombie, Johnson, Erskine.*

"Furs on Ice" was released on a live record called *Abercrombie, Johnson, Erskine,* on ECM records. It's one of my favorites. I saw a few gigs from this tour, and I have to say that the song "Furs on Ice" was a highlight of every night. When the ECM recording came out in 1989, I wore it out. To my ears, it was a continuation of the type of interplay started in 1961 by the Bill Evans trio with Scott LaFaro and Paul Motian, and the later Jim Hall Trio with Don Thompson and Terry Clarke. So when Peter told me that he had the whole tour recorded on DAT tape, I freaked out. His recordings include a few different versions of "Furs on Ice" and it's drum solo, so including an alternate version of this amazing tune is a thrill for us at Legends.

For transcriptions and Peter's commentary on these tunes, go to the Transcription section of this Legends book.

Additional digital downloadable bonus tracks and play-alongs are also included. Access the digital dowload code on page 1.

Rob Shanahan

—LOOKING

1978 A New Horizon

By Gary Farmer

It was surprising but I felt immediately at home. We enjoyed playing together instantly." states drummer Peter Erskine.

For those few who haven't heard. Erskine has indeed found a new home, playing with the jazz-rock quartet Weather Report. The group members include Josef Zawinul. keyboards: Wayne Shorter, saxophone and Jaco Pastorius, electric bass.

The move came suddenly when, according to Erskine, "I was in Miami and Jaco and Joe played some of the Heavy Weather tapes. The music was fantastic. They were looking for a drummer and after hearing me play only once, I was invited to join the group. It was a gamble on their part, but my musical style and personality appealed to them." Erskine has already done some work on Weather Report's latest album, Mr. Gone. Currently. The group is preparing for their US tour which will commence in Washington D.C.

The format of Weather Report is a drastic change for Erskine, whose previous experience included three years with the Stan Kenton Orchestra and two years with Maynard Ferguson's 18-piece band. Though Erskine says his work with Weather Report will keep him "very busy." he anticipates a less grueling schedule than the constant one-nighters he experienced with the Ferguson band.

GF: How about starting off with some details of your childhood.

PE: I was born in 1954, in Somers Point, New Jersey. My father was a musician. I was exposed to music at an early age. My mother always appreciated music, and her interest grew along with mine. Now she can tell me who's playing drums on certain records. She recognizes Billy Cobham's drumming from Elvin Jones, which is hip because she never liked drummers. She never liked Kenton either, which is funny because I ended up working for him.

I started drum lessons when I was five years old. My first teacher was Johnny Civera, who played drums for Patti Page and Billy May. He was a patient man and gave me a solid musical foundation. He also introduced me to the Stan Kenton clinics, and with some additional prodding from my father, it was the start of a long association. I went to his clinic for several years. I got exposed to some very talented musicians like Ron Carter, Alan Dawson, Charley Perry, Ed Soph, Dee Barton and the Kenton bands. It was a tremendous experience. During the school year I'd play along with a lot of records and try to hear as many different groups as possible.

GF: What type of groups?

PE: I listened to a lot of big bands. Art Blakey was one of the first drummers I listened to, although he worked mostly with smaller groups. I was listening to people like Grady Tate and Elvin. My sister used to date jazz musicians and a lot of records would end up at the house. I was lucky to be able to hear all those things. I went to Interlochen Arts Academy in Michigan for three years. It's a high school with an emphasis on the arts. I met a lot of good people there.

Later, I studied classical percussion with Billy Dorn, who was the mallet player for Toscannini and the NBC Symphony. But I really learned a lot from Dave Sporny. He used to sing drum licks and fills. Hearing that was good for basic big band playing. I also went to Indiana University for one year and studied with George Gaber. That summer, I worked some clubs in Atlantic City, New Jersey, playing timpani for the Ice Capades. I got a call from Stan Kenton, who wanted me to play with the band at the Newport Festival in Lincoln Center. I sat in during a rehearsal. June Christy was singing with the band that evening and they thought I was her drummer. I went

BACK

in and sight read some of her charts. Later, Stan came up to me, gave me a couple of albums and told me to meet him in Ohio in a week. I didn't go back to school. Just picked up my suitcase and drums, travelled with the band for two days and studied the albums.

GF: What kind of drums did you start out with?

PE: I had this little set with a Chinese tom-tom and a funky old cymbal. Later, I graduated to a Gretsch set, a red sparkle that had two bunny rabbit decals on the bass drum head. The set had a snare drum, small tom, bass, and a couple of cymbals. I added a floor tom that was actually a Slingerland marching drum that someone had attached legs to. I had those drums for quite a while. In high school, I bought a blond, wood Ludwig set. I had a very bastardized set when I joined the Kenton band. A Rogers snare, Ludwig set, Sonor pedals and Slingerland stands.

One time, I was with Stan in Chicago and the damn pedal I was using literally exploded. Springs were flying out of it and everything fell apart. Brad Morey of Slingerland was there and told me that would never happen if I played Slingerland. The folks from Slingerland came out and brought me a hi-hat stand. Slingerland and I were touch and go for awhile, but after the European tour with the Kenton band, my drums were beat up, and they were nice enough to give me a new set. That was the beginning of my association with Slingerland.

Peter at 7 years of age, final concert of Kenton Stage Band Camp at IU (1961)

F.A. Erskine, M.D.

GF: What are you currently using?

PE: I've experimented with a lot of different sizes, from a relatively small kit with a 20" bass, up to a 24." Now, with Weather Report, my set consists of a 22" bass, 8 X 12 and 9 X 13 mounted toms, a 16 X 16 floor tom, a 10" Roto-tom and a 5 1/2 X 14 brass shell snare. The snare is a combination gut and wire and produces a fantastic sound! I use CS Black Dot heads except on the snare which has an Ambassador head.

GF: Any special considerations regarding your set-up?

PE: I kind of evolved since the Kenton band, putting the swish cymbal down by the tom-toms. I used to play it up higher, and play the ride cymbal lower and flatter. My cymbal set-up includes a 14" Rock hi hat, 22" ride-crash on the left, 22" Ping ride, 22" Swish, 20" crash and a 13" crash that's paper thin. All my cymbals are Zildjian. I'm also getting into wind chimes, wood blocks and gongs. I also use a small triangle.

GF: Have you played left-handed cymbal?

PE: A little bit. If you have the right frame of mind you can master anything in drumming quite easily. There's no magic to learning the instrument. There are some endowed people and that is what makes artists out of musicians. If someone has the desire, puts in the time, and listens, he can groove. It's a matter of what you're exposed to and when you get a chance to play.

GF: You use a wooden tip 5A stick?

1961, Indiana University (Bloomington, IN) at summer jazz camp with Louis Hayes

F.A. Erskine, M.D.

PE: Yes, and Slingerland has just put my name on them. I think they get a nicer sound from a cymbal. I used the plastic tipped sticks on a couple of things but I much prefer the sound obtained with the wood tip.

GF: How do you feel about multiple drum set-ups?

PE: A lot of drums are nice. On the New Vintage album I did with Maynard I used my standard set-up, plus I rented a couple of small concert toms. An 8" and 10". It was fun to play but I think I sounded like a kid. Whenever I got an opportunity to do a fill, I did. It was like a new toy. I guess it depends on where your head is at musically.

GF: Have you done any double bass drum work?

PE: No, but I'd like to try it someday. I've seen Jack DeJonette with a fairly large set as well as a small one, and he sounds great on both. I've also seen a lot of kids with multiple drum set-ups that didn't know beans about playing the ride cymbal. The fact that you have all those drums doesn't do much musically.

GF: Any concepts on tuning drums?

PE: I used single heads for awhile but I prefer the sound of the drum with two heads. It has some tone to it. Mel Lewis gave me a hard time once when I was with Kenton. He said, "You should be using both heads on those drums." With that influence and the advice of my teacher, I started thinking about it. I started to really listen to the drums and the two-headed drum sounds terrific. I use a 5-ply Slingerland with no mufflers. I don't like to muffle the drums at all. I try to get as much of the tone as I can. Muffling is like playing a violin with a mute on it all the time. You can always muffle a drum if you want to, but in most playing situations, if you're dealing with volumes, you don't want too much muffling.

GF: Are you interested in electronic drumming?

PE: A little bit. I was very impressed with the Syndrum that Joe Pollard makes. The Moog drum seems interesting too. I'd like to work with a drum through an Echo-Plex someday. I think that would be interesting. I have no experience working with electronic drums, though in college we did experiment with phase shifting.

GF: Do you feel reading is important?

PE: I did a lot of reading in school, and I like to read. I would encourage any drummer to read as much as he can. If you're serious about playing professionally, you've got to read. You can get anything thrown at you. Reading should be like reading a book. You don't have to stop and spell the word and in music you shouldn't have to stop and count by using your fingers. Eventually, it should become automatic.

"If you have the right frame of mind you can master anything in drumming quite easily. There's no magic to learning the instrument....If someone has the desire, puts in the time, and listens, they can groove."

GF: Do you still practice?

PE: When I get the chance. I try to practice when I'm home on vacation. Practicing is important. It's something that takes great discipline. I did a lot of it when I was younger.

GF: Do you enjoy it?

PE: Yes, but you get into a lot of bad habits on the road. It's easy to get out of the routine of practicing. When I left Kenton I went back to school to study with George Gaber. He was alarmed at what my hands were doing. I put a lot of effort into the drum rather than bringing the sound out of the drum. I play very hard and I think I could work on lightening up a bit. That's what I'm trying to do.

GF: Though you don't practice as often as you'd like, what would an ideal practice routine consist of?

PE: When I work on the snare drum, I try to get my hands in good shape. When I was working on the matched grip I concentrated on stick height, angle and feel. When I'm practicing on the set, I try to practice basic timekeeping. Every so often I'll play around the drums.

GF: Would you suggest practicing on the pads, or a set?

PE: Both. I think practicing on a pad is good because you can work on wrists and hands. You're not driving everybody nuts with the loud, distracting sound of the drum. On a pad, you can get a very objective look at how you sound and how you're playing. But I like practicing on a drum set, getting a cymbal feel going. Part of playing on a drum set is getting a sound out of it.

GF: Have you ever tried a practice pad set?

PE: Yes. They're pretty good, but I like to see a drummer practice as much as he can on a drum set. I never had a practice set, but I've always meant to buy one. I think they'd be good for working on independence. What's more important is the sound you get out of your instrument. The music you make. The feeling, the groove that happens. The mere technical end of drumming doesn't interest me that much.

GF: You're more into the sound aspect?

PE: I'm technically oriented to some degree. I've got a fair amount of speed, but that's just like a trumpet player trying to play high, or a drummer trying to play fast. Buddy can play more than just fast — and swing. Maynard can do more than just play high. It's something they're noted for, but it doesn't nearly do them justice as musicians. Young musicians get seduced by the extravagance available on an instrument.

GF: Do you teach at all?

PE: Yes, when I'm in one place. I like teaching very much. I did a lot of teaching when I was with the Kenton band, doing the clinics. I find it rewarding. People were generous with their time with me when I was younger and I like returning that. I try to stress to a player that he may practice all over his drums for three hours, but might accomplish more working on his ride cymbal for ten minutes. You can play all day on the drum set if you want to, but you can accomplish more in ten minutes of good practice as opposed to two hours of wasteful practice. The amount of time isn't necessarily important.

GF: What are your thoughts regarding drum soloing?

PE: A solo should be a musical extension of what's come before in the music and a preview of what will come next. You should try to tell a story. A mere display of chops is fine, but music is music and a solo should tell a story, and be well constructed. We all fall into the trap of trying to play fast and amazing. But I try to keep it musical. The success of that lies with the listener.

> "A solo should be a musical extension of what's come before in the music, and a preview of what will come next. You should try and tell a story. A mere display of chops is fine but music is music and a solo should tell a story, and be well constructed."

GF: Do you have any favorite soloists?

PE: I love Elvin Jones and Jack DeJohnette. Billy did some exciting drumming on *Crosswinds*. I dig Roy Haynes a lot. I listen to a lot of bop and horn players too. Sometimes when I'm soloing, I'll even pull a cheap trick and play a bop head, like "*Billy's Bounce*" or "*Duke's Place*." Music is melody, harmony and most important, rhythm.

GF: Of all the people you worked with, do you have any favorites?

PE: Stan was like my musical father. I learned a lot with that band, playing every night. That's a very maturing kind of thing, working every night with other musicians. You've got audiences to deal with and your own conception of what music is. When I joined Stan, I was heading in a different direction musically; the Mahavishnu Orchestra had just appeared on the scene and I started to listen to all those things. I had to get more jazz roots together. It was a blessing I was put out there, to learn slowly what jazz drumming was about. I learned the importance of a ride cymbal and getting a groove going. When I was with Maynard, Gordon Johnson and Biff Hannon taught me so much in regards to playing and preparation. I valued their help immensely. Of course, working with Weather Report is fantastic. It's a very creative environment. The work is demanding and if I'm not playing it, then I'll accept the challenge and learn. I know with this group it's going to get better and better.

GF: Is there one individual you would credit as being the most influential drummer over the past twenty years?

Norman Seeff, WR promo (CBS)

PE: I'd have to name a few. Max Roach was very important and Philly Joe was a great bop drummer. Jo Jones did so much. Tony Williams has given a great deal to drumming. Listen to some of the playing he did with Miles. They fed off each other. Drummers gain from each other and from other musicians. It's a revolving kind of thing.

GF: Do you feel you're still growing musically? What are your goals for the future?

PE: I hope I'm still growing. Just playing new things, listening to tapes and records, or talking to people. I'd like to get into writing. There's a lot more to music that I'd like to explore. I know with Weather Report I'll have that freedom. I think this is what I'll be doing for a long time.

GF: Any words of advice to offer an aspiring drummer?

PE: Yes, don't be late to your gig. Keep your ears open. Enjoy the music and have fun when you play. Be versatile. My experience in big band prepared me for different musical situations. And, give it everything you have because music is a groovy thing. If one person walks away happy from what you've played, it's a great thing. You can't do that selling shoes.

Peter Erskine
1983 On The Cover

By Rick Mattingly

If Peter Erskine isn't careful, he's going to start giving jazz, musicians a good name. I mean, we all know about the reputation jazz players have with the general public, right? The stereotypical jazzer is perceived to be a sullen, somber and solitary figure. You can spot jazz musicians immediately: they tend to look melancholy, undernourished, and their eyes have the look of those who are more at home in dimly lit, smoke filled nightclubs than out in the sunshine and fresh air. So what's with this guy Erskine? How dare he be so healthy; so positive; so happy. If the average person were to encounter a smiling Peter Erskine bopping down the sidewalk in his baseball cap, I doubt if it would occur to that person that Peter is a jazz musician. There's just something too wholesome about him. Doesn't he care about his image?

To hell with image—all that matters is how he plays. When you hear Peter Erskine play, you are hearing a jazz musician. First coming to prominence with Stan Kenton—whose band Peter joined at the age of eighteen—Erskine quickly established himself as a solid and confident player. After three years with Kenton, Peter enrolled at Indiana University, but within a year, was back on the road, this time with Maynard Ferguson. Following his two-year stint with the Ferguson band, Peter turned up in Weather Report, where he was to remain for the next four years. (Peter now holds the record for longevity by a drummer in Weather Report.) During his tenure in that group, Peter began turning up with a variety of small jazz groups, both in clubs and on record. One of these groups was Steps, and when the members of that group decided to make a commitment to each other, Peter left Weather Report and moved to New York. Since that time, Peter has been touring with Steps and working with them to prepare for their first U.S. recording.

Meanwhile, he has recorded his own first album as a leader. The record, to be released this month, features Michael and Randy Brecker, Mike Mainieri, Don Alias, Eddie Gomez, Don Grolnick, Bob Mintzer and Kenny Kirkland. The music on the album, and the music he is playing with Steps, is mainstream jazz, and Peter couldn't be happier about that.

RM: I think you surprised a lot of people when you joined Weather Report because you were already somewhat typecast as a big band drummer.

PE: Yeah, I guess so. It's funny, because when I joined Kenton's band, I was not listening to big band music at that time. I was in college and had been listening a lot to things like Miles Davis' *Bitches Brew*, The Mahavishnu Orchestra, who had just come out, and Weather Report, who had come out with their first album about a year before. In fact, I was listening to the second Weather Report album when I got the call from Kenton. So even though I wasn't really thinking of doing that kind of thing at the time, I had grown up listening to big band music, and it excited this thing that was inside me. I think any kind of a gig that a drummer can take that has strong traditions built into it is an invaluable kind of learning experience. And I did have a lot to learn when I joined Kenton's group. So I got into the big band thing, never really thinking of myself so much as the "typical" big band player. I was trying to improve the way I played, and I really admired the great big band drummers and the way they carried the band. But I would always find myself feeling a little envious when I would hear small-group drummers—guys who really played the stuff. I would think, "*That's* the kind of drumming I *really* want to play."

Kenton's band, and Maynard's band to a lesser degree, were both kind of heavy. I think my touch was kind of heavy to begin with and so it sort of remained that way. I got fast, but I was still hitting the drums pretty hard. When those bands would play opposite other bands, like when I heard Ed Soph play with Woody Herman's band, I saw how light he was playing and how fleet he was moving. I thought, "That's more the kind of thing I would like to do, and I would like to be thought of as that kind of player."

RM: So did you ever feel, yourself, that you were getting typecast?

PE: No, I wasn't really worrying about it. People tend to try and put a label on most things that they see or hear. It makes it more comfortable for them. They do it with music, with musicians, and with all the popular arts. I don't think the artists think that way themselves. People always have a different conception of themselves than how others perceive them to be. Of course, you have to get some sort of impression across to the public. But the way I considered it—and still do—was that I knew I was young and still learning and I wasn't close to the point where I was going to get to.

When I joined Weather Report, the first concerts were in Japan, and when we got there, they had a big press conference. The Japanese are incredibly avid followers of jazz, and they really knew the history of Weather Report. So one of the central points of this press conference was the new drummer. A guy stood up and asked me, "What makes you think, having

Weather Report press conference 1978

Shigeru Uchiyama

played with Stan Kenton and Maynard Ferguson, that you're qualified to play with Weather Report?" I was thinking, "Geeze, gimme a break. I haven't even played the first gig yet." And so I got into this meandering thing about, "Well, good music is good music, and requires the same type thing…" Joe Zawinul interrupted me and said to the guy, "What are you talking about? Weather Report *is* like a big band. The sound is big and we play like a bunch of guys and it's a small group too…"

The basic prerequisites are the same. The most outstanding feature, I think, of Weather Report is the conceptual framework of the group. It's a really incredible combination of extremely modern music, very tonal music, and rhythmic music. To me, it was a natural next step, and apparently, from what they'd heard of me, they felt it would be a natural next step too. Kenton had a lot of tradition. Maynard's thing was not so traditionally bound. People would hate the band a lot of times because Maynard would be playing all these rock things. I always thought the best thing we did with Maynard's band were the older bebop charts; that's when the band really shined.

RM: A lot of people just knew the band from "Rocky."

PE: I think any time a jazz band gets a hit like that, no one should begrudge that particular artist the success. People like Maynard, Chuck Mangione, and Bob James lured a lot of people into the jazz department in record stores, who normally wouldn't have browsed around there too much. And I know first hand that a lot of people got turned on to Weather Report, Miles Davis, Charlie Parker and other things because they heard a Chuck Mangione record. They would go to a record store and ask, "What else do you have that's jazz?" They thought that was jazz.

So anyway, that was an exciting thing for Maynard, but I think it steered him in a bit of a funny direction. He started going after more and more movie-theme hits. It's an objective with what you want to do with your music, but you can't try to play music with the sole purpose of having a hit. It seems that kind of thinking is doomed, sooner or later. I think the most important thing is to make the best music you can. If it's really good, it will find its way to people. Doing themes to all sorts of TV shows and stuff is really underestimating the listeners' intelligence. The artist's real audience deserves more than that. You want to play for a lot of people, but you do have a faithful audience of listeners. You can't expect them to continue to more or less support you if you cast aside your musical integrity. That's the dilemma of trying to be commercial.

Weather Report never tried to be commercial. It's amazingly unique that Weather Report is as popular as it is, and yet doesn't try to be anything other than what it is. They don't worry about fulfilling expectations of other people. It creates its own music and continues to have lasting value because the band doesn't try to achieve anything other than its own creative evolution. Weather Report is my favorite band. It always has been; it always will be. I was very fortunate; it was one of those "right place at the right time" kind of things. It opened an incredible number of doors for me, too, to be able to play with other jazz musicians. When I was

> "I was very fortunate; it was one of those "right place at the right time" kind of things. It opened an incredible number of doors for me."

living in Los Angeles and when I played outside the context of Weather Report, I gradually built a reputation for being a small-group player. I really enjoyed working with people like George Cables, Freddie Hubbard, Joe Farrell, Bobby Hutcherson and Joe Henderson.

RM: Except for "Dry Cleaner From Des Moines."

PE: Yeah, "Dry Cleaner" is kind of a bright little number. Originally she tried recording it as a bebop tune. Then I was messing around with that little brush beat and the producer came rushing in and said, "Yeah! Keep doing that." Then Jaco walked in, made up the bass thing, and we cut the basic track. Then Joni came in and sang on top of it. That was like an impromptu thing; it was fun. I was really knocked out to to be playing on a Joni Mitchell album. From a jazz stand point, I don't know if it captured the Mingus musical mood, but that wasn't the point. It was Joni's approach to that music and her

Peter with the Stan Kenton Orchestra age 18.

Peter Erskine Library

RM: One of the first things you did outside of Weather Report was the Joni Mitchell album, Mingus.

PE: We did that real quick—two afternoon sessions; first takes. It's a good record, although when I listen to that album now I find the mood a little depressing.

collaboration with Mingus, and, you know…

RM: That's what came out of it.

PE: Yeah. I think it should be listened to a little more in that context. A lot of people got real uptight and said, "Jaco was totally the wrong bass player for that." That wasn't the point. It wasn't trying to be a Mingus Dynasty with vocals.

RM: I saw a review that said, "It sounds sort of like Weather Report with a girl singer."

PE: Awww…reviews! You know, there are some really knowledgeable writers out there about jazz; the ones who have constructive criticisms about the music. You really appreciate that. I don't like to get defensive about reviews. We've all had our share of ghastly reviews. People, for some reason, may really not like you. Basically, if a writer has a good musical comment, I can read it and say, "Yeah, he's right." Like one writer was writing about Weather Report and said that I had a tendency to overplay, and I should watch that. And I thought, "Yeah, he's got a point." But another guy once said, "As for the drummer, I can think of 500 other drummers I'd rather listen to before I listen to Peter Erskine." What a thing to say! I mean, I can't even *think* of 500 drummers. Hyperbole is sometimes useful, but that's like doubting the intelligence of everyone. We're not total fools.

When we're playing, some things don't work and some things don't sound so good, but if the writer respects music and musicians at all, he's got to give a little credit to those musicians. I'm not saying that they should blandly say, "Everything is great." But at the same time, jazz musicians aren't trying to put scams over on people, and I don't appreciate it when a reviewer tries to take away from the obvious craft that's in something. I always thought a lot of jazz writers got into this "Broadway reviewer" mentality of "Let's close the show down" kind of thing. That doesn't help anybody. Some people try to build names for themselves by writing strongly worded diatribes against certain players. That's pretty worthless musical criticism. If jazz writers really love the music, they should support it. Keep artistic integrity in there and keep the standards high, but be objective and realize that there are a lot of tastes. There are a lot of musicians and a lot of people listening, and we've all got to support it if we love it. I once heard jazz critic and writer Ira Gitler speak, and he said that all the jazz musicians he had ever known have been banner carriers for the music, in the way they thought they could best do it. One of the remarkable things about jazz is the love in the music. I think listeners can hear that love, and feel the commitment. I think that's what makes it special. So if we love it the way we say we do, the main thing is to keep it alive somehow.

"One of the remarkable things about jazz is the love in the music. I think listeners can hear that love, and feel the commitment."

RM: That brings us to the records you've done on Contemporary Records—a label that's certainly doing its part to keep jazz alive. You did albums with Joe Farrell, Joe Henderson, George Cables . . .

PE: George Cables is an amazing musician. We have a

real natural affinity. I worked with him in a club in L.A. one night, just kind of by accident, and after that we started playing together. I really like his tunes and I love playing with him. That basic rhythm section—George, Tony Dumas and I—also did the Joe Farrell album, and went to Japan with Freddie Hubbard.

The Joe Henderson album was interesting. I played with Chick Corea on some of the cuts. It's a good record, but I wish I'd played better. I was amazingly uptight that day. My car engine blew up on the San Diego Freeway on the way to do the session. So somebody had to come and pick me up on the side of the freeway and take me to the studio. But it was good. I hope I get to play with Joe and Chick again.

John Koenig is putting out excellent records on the Contemporary label. The sound is a good, intimate jazz sound, and the music is happening. All the stuff is done in a matter of two or three days. That's the way I like jazz records. The last Weather Report album—the mixing took two or three months, but the basic tracks were done in two afternoons. I like the immediacy; that's what jazz is all about. I like the multi-track technology, and I love what the studios can do, but there's something about recording direct to two-track—you can't beat it! Just that spirit of, "Let's go for it and do it!" If you get good players, you can do it. So I like the spirit

Peter Erskine Library

of the records that Contemporary is putting out. A good jazz label.

RM: Did you do any studio work while you were in California?

PE: I did a few movies and a couple of TV shows. I wasn't tearing up the studio scene by any means. It's a different art doing studio playing and getting a good recorded sound. There are some musicians who are really amazing at it, and I really respect that. But I decided at some point that I didn't want to be a "record-date drummer." I don't want to be on just anybody's record. I figure when you make a record, it's going to be around for a long time, so you want it to stand for something. I like to have a certain intent on a record; I like it to at least be going for something that I like or appreciate, or to be with musicians who I like to play with. So I don't do a bunch of record dates.

As far as anonymous studio work is concerned, I welcome it to a point. But that stuff drives you crazy after a while. I like movie dates; they're really challenging. You get a 60-piece orchestra in there, you've got the clock, the pressure's really on, you can't make mistakes—I like that. Some people just take it in stride, but you could tell that I was more or less new at it because I would go into the booth and listen to the playbacks. I was trying to learn how to get a better sound in those situations. I like going to the movies, so playing on soundtracks was a kick. I've played on a lot of soundtracks for the kind of movies they wind up showing at drive-ins as the second feature.

RM: Would you like to tell me the names of any of those, so our readers…

PE: [laughing] No, please! I dragged my girl friend to a couple, just to sit there and listen to the drums mixed way back behind some tire squeals or something. "Listen! That's *me!*" She got pretty tired of that. After a while, if you do too much of that sort of thing, it starts affecting your life. I like to do some studio work, but what I've done is very little compared to the people who do it for a living. I like to do just enough for the challenge, and the sport of it. It's a kick.

But I want to be a jazz musician. That's what I really want to do, and I'm fortunate enough right now that I'm *really* happy with the music I'm playing. I want it to get better and I know it's going to get better, but I go to bed at night thinking, "I'm playing the music I want to play." I think everyone should be able to do the recording thing, and be well-versed enough to play that kind of stuff. Being a professional musician demands that— especially now, for drummers.

You can't just say, "I want to be a jazz drummer" right off and expect to work. You've got to do casuals, you've got to play dances, you've got to play record dates, you get calls for jingles, you get called to be funky— you've got to do it. It's not exactly paying your dues, but it's a way of being heard by more and more people.

"I want to be a jazz musician. That's what I really want to do, and I'm fortunate enough right now that I'm *really* happy with the music I'm playing."

Drummers today have to be more eclectic than they used to be. Right now, I'm trying to synthesize all the musical things I love and forge them into some kind of style. If Steps makes it, God willing, then I'll have the setting in which I can do that. That's all you can ask for, really.

RM: A moment ago, you mentioned that you love

studio technology, but that you also like recording direct, with the whole band. What is it you like about each situation?

PE: It takes real skill to be able to put drums on top of a track that's already there, or play drums to a click track. You have to make the music happen to this existing track, or this metronome. It takes a fair amount of experience, and you've got to keep your ears wide open to be able to fit yourself into it. With the creative process, you can take amazing advantage of the overdub situation.

With Weather Report, we would sometimes put a lot of different drum tracks on top of each other. Sonically, it created a whole different sound perspective. We weren't doing it because it was the only way we could

1962, playing with Donald Byrd (Indiana University)

F.A. Erskine, M.D.

get those rhythms. It was just different. When you record things separately, you can bring certain things out. I'm going to try doing some things live with the Oberheim drum machine. It will essentially be me playing along with myself, because I will have programmed the machine. I like playing off of things that are already there. The overdub thing can be creative, and can be good.

However, you can kill the spirit of live music if you're not careful. You start hearing all the things you want to perfect, and you get caught up in just that thing of overdubbing, and you can end up with just a polished nothing. I like the live to two-track thing more, but still, the potential in multitrack is great. I think what's happening now with synthesizers and computers and all this stuff is wild. Nothing's ever going to replace acoustic instruments, but this other stuff is neat too. I dig it. I dig the whole thing.

RM: Do you ever feel that the emphasis right now is on technology rather than music?

PE: Perhaps. It could just be growing pains. For a while, the emphasis is going to be on the technical part of something. It's like certain movies which have amazing technical effects, but don't have a story that moves people. With records, the producer and the artist have to say, "Well, this *sounds* amazing, but what's most important here?" I've seen a lot of records sort of floundering between creativity and technology. Creativity takes a good, strong overview, and takes some discipline. So you've got to be able to use these tools creatively. There's nothing wrong with the tools, whether they be a hammer and nails or a 24-track recording machine and a synthesizer. It's up to *us* to use the stuff intelligently.

RM: From what you hear, do you think enough people *are* using the stuff intelligently?

PE: I don't know if there are enough. I don't know how intelligent people are either—look how many people are shooting each other. I listen less and less to records now. When I joined Weather Report, I had a bunch of tapes, and Jaco told me, "In a couple of years, you're not going to be listening to any of that shit." He was sort of saying that the music we were going to be playing was going to be so heavy that I wouldn't want to listen to anything else. Now, I haven't taken that to heart, because when I was young, I was told, "Listen to every kind of music." And you have to. You have to keep your ears wide open. But you can't listen to just anything, because a lot of the records coming out are like certain types of food—you get no nourishment from them, and they can actually be bad for you. So in that way, yeah, a lot of people aren't using the stuff creatively. But like I said, all of this technology can be taken advantage of and used. It comes from a knowledge of music. If you don't know what you're doing, it will come out sounding like a big piece of nothing. A lot of music sounds good, but there is no substance. It's just like cotton candy.

RM: You mentioned using an Oberheim drum machine, and I notice you've got one here in your apartment.

PE: I had my first experience with one of the so-called drum computers using Roger Linn's machine. I programmed it to play the form of Wayne Shorter's tune, "When It Was Now," on the Weather Report album. I was programming while they were practicing their parts, so when I was finished, they were ready to do a take. The tape started rolling, I pushed a button, the guys played along with the machine, and I played claves or something, just jamming along with the machine. And that first take was what we used on the album.

First of all, I think they are a fantastic tool for a writer, because he can get an idea of what a tune will sound like in the privacy of his own home. With a synthesizer, a drum machine and one of those little multi-track tape recorders, a composer can, in about an hour's time, get a tune in pretty good rough shape. I'm using the Oberheim

DMX for that very purpose. I'm starting to compose more and more, so I can get a studio-quality drum sound along with the synthesizer and get a good working tape with which to do further exploration or work.

I don't think there's any real valid argument that drum machines are going to put drummers out of business, any more than synthesizers have put other musicians out of work. People who are using them in the studios are hiring drummers to program the machines. Drum machines are used because they are their own unique instrument. Some people like the sound of them and they like the process of creating the drum part in this multi-track sense from the ground up. And after they get it the way they want it, it's consistent—it's always there.

RM: How did the other members of Weather Report feel about playing along with a machine?

PE: They liked it. It was a different groove, and for that particular tune it worked well. The band was used to working with sequencers, and in essence, that's what a drum computer is. It's a very sophisticated sequencer with real drum sounds, digitally stored.

I like to think about the potential for using it live. It can serve as an accompaniment to my playing, or I can trigger it with some kind of trigger system. For example, with my little 18" bass drum, I might trigger the bass drum sound that's in the machine. All of a sudden, in the middle of a show, I could have this fat, studio-sound bass drum, instead of just having this one jazz sound. It might permit more sound possibilities live as well as in the recorded context. Right now, I'm working with Oberheim to improve the sounds they have.

On the one hand, I'm intrigued with that stuff; I like electronics and I'm very fascinated by the electronic age. On the other hand, like when I went down to the NAMM show last summer, I thought I would be excited by all the electronic toys. But it was just the opposite. What was turning me on were the drums at the Yamaha booth, Gary Gauger's RIMS system, and the pre-tuned stuff that Remo had. *That* is what got me really excited: acoustical instruments pushing air. When you really get down to it, there's no substitute for the sound of an instrument moving air to a pair of ears. That's what music is really about. The capabilities of computers hold a lot of promise, but I'd still rather hear Elvin hit a drum than hear anybody push a button.

RM: One of the main complaints about the machines is that they're *too* perfect.

PE: Yeah, well you can get around that. The machines do permit the human element to be in there if you know how to program it. Otherwise, if you rely on the automatic clock mechanism, it's going to auto/correct to the nearest 16th or whatever. So with patience, you can create something that's close to human. Computers can do certain functions that a human could never do, but yet, the subtleties of human thought are just too complex to program into a computer. The mistake people make is expecting the drum machine to be like a drummer. It's not. It's just a machine that records rhythmic patterns. I think the idea of a computer drum machine is great though. In my little apartment, I can put a drum track down so I can hear what a tune is going to sound like. And I'm certainly not putting any drummers out of work. It's just much easier for me to get the stuff together on tape. And it's fun! I've come up with some different beats using the Oberheim. It's a different way of approaching rhythms.

When I was in Weather Report, Joe and I had this scheme worked out where we were each going to have an Oberheim drum machine. Then by means of cassette interface, we were going to send ideas to each other on cassette, play them back on our own machine, and see what the other one had come up with. That was going to be our long-distance way of rehearsing new stuff when I was in New York.

"When you really get down to it, there's no substitute for the sound of an instrument moving air to a pair of ears."

RM: Let's move from drum machines to the real thing. You've been using Yamaha for the last couple of years.

PE: Going to Japan on several occasions gave me the opportunity to play Yamaha, and I was perfectly delighted with them. The craftsmanship on the shells is about as good as you could ask for. They keep their round and the heads sit perfectly on the shells; there are no funny bumps where there shouldn't be. I don't know exactly what the physics are; all I know is that they sound really good. A lot of people have commented on the warmth they hear from my drums.

The hardware is tremendously designed. Their lighter weight hardware is more than adequate for my needs. Also, it's easier to haul around and work with on the bandstand. And nothing has ever gone wrong with any of my Yamaha hardware yet.

RM: I think a lot of people are somewhat suspicious of endorsements nowadays. A lot of drummers jump around from company to company, and people start to wonder if the artist really cares about the instrument, or if it's just another business deal.

PE: The drum companies have been pretty generous with a great number of artists. As a practical business thing for the companies, it gets their instruments out there where they're seen by a lot of people. And in its best role, the artist is providing a very good service for the drum company by providing invaluable feedback about the instrument. The endorsees will be the first to get hold of a new thing, so they can give the feedback of "This is good; this is not so good." So the endorsement thing makes good sense for the companies. They're giving away a lot, but I think they're getting it back. It's a gamble. I think some of us make better endorsers than others. Some guys endorse something and then turn around and hock what they've been given. Or then there was this drummer who was with one of the large drum companies. He became a great embarassment because he turned up in one of the so-called "men's magazines," and he was talking about all sorts of distasteful stuff. The whole endorsement idea is aimed at the young market; it's to get the kids to buy the big drumsets. And here's someone who totally abused the responsibility he was supposed to have with that. It showed a total lack of sensitivity to his role of being a role model for young people, which is what you are when you endorse something.

There's a lot of jumping around in the endorsement thing too. If anyone cares to look through the past few years of *Modern Drummer*, they'll see a lot of the same faces appearing behind a lot of different drums. Everyone has their reasons. Maybe they're searching for the instrument they have the best rapport with. But I think the way some of the guys jumped around all over the place made their endorsement mean less.

I thought very seriously before I changed my endorsement because I was very conscious of that. But I just finally felt that I had to follow my integrity in terms of the instrument I wanted to play, and Yamaha drums seemed to come closer to the ideal of what I wanted to play on. So I kind of feel like a company man. They've been generous enough to let me use an instrument that's really terrific. I hope they feel that I provide a service for them in return, in terms of promoting their product, speaking well about it, and giving feedback to them.

The Zildjians have also been tremendously generous and helpful. I have a set of cymbals now that are totally incredible: 14" New Beat hi-hats, an 18" flat ride, a 17" crash, a 16" swish, a 10" splash, and a 20"K ride—one of the new K's made in Boston.

A few years ago, I endorsed a couple of things in the electronic percussion realm that I don't really use any more. For a second, I thought I was getting carried away and putting my name on too many things. Sure, it doesn't hurt, and I got a lot of exposure. Somehow, Maynard's band really attracted a lot of endorsement opportunities. It's very flattering when you're young in the business and all of a sudden you're getting your picture all over the place. But eventually, I was getting tired of seeing all those ads, so I put somewhat of a moratorium on it for a while. Now I just stick to the basics: Yamaha drums, Zildjian cymbals, Remo heads and Vic Firth sticks.

Weather Report rehearsal 1978

Shigeru Uchiyama

RM: Over the years, your drums and cymbals have gotten smaller.

PE: My touch has lightened up. I'm playing a lighter drum head, using lighter sticks, playing smaller cymbals and smaller drums. I like the tone quality I'm getting now. I feel like I'm just discovering how to hit a drum. When I was with Kenton's band, I used to always break cymbals. I don't think I was hitting them right. But now I don't break them. I don't break drumheads like I used to, or sticks. I'm lightening up my playing; getting a nice sound.

I used to beat the sound into the instrument more than get it out. It's just understanding what the instrument is supposed to sound like. It's funny—a lot of the stuff my teacher, George Gaber, told me ten years ago is just starting to register. Sometimes I think, "Geeze, I wish I'd known what he was talking about back then." But you can't. You just have to trust that as you get older, you'll put one and one together and figure out what they were talking about all along.

I don't mind playing larger drums, but that "big drumset" thing, to me, is kind of outdated. At the NAMM show, I saw these huge drumsets, which may appeal to a certain market, but there's nothing in that for me. The stuff seems overblown, and I've played some pretty big drumsets in my time. Some guys do use them very well. Steve Smith has a big double-bass set, and he sounds great. But for me, personally, I feel kind of intimidated when I get behind a big set of drums. I'm not inspired to start hitting them. I really like the small sets. Over at the Gretsch exhibit, they had a ton of big drumsets, but they had one little jazz set—18" bass, 12" and 14" tom-toms—and that was great. *Those* are the drums, right there. I love my Yamaha drums, and I'm a company man when it comes to those matters, but someday I'm going to get myself a little Gretsch jazz drumset. I think every jazz drummer should have one. Have it sitting over by the fireplace and on those inspired evenings play a couple of Tony Williams licks.

One thing I was very distressed to see at the show—a lot of companies are drilling big holes in their drums. I don't understand these "cutaway" drums. I guess it's a gimmick to get people to buy drums. I don't want to sell the r&d technology short, but I don't really think that's what a drum is all about. It was a little distressing to me to see drums that were missing half of their thing. All these drums butchered—that turned me off.

RM: When you were with Kenton, didn't you use single-headed drums?

PE: Yeah. I went to single head because they had more of that dry, "chunky" rock sound. When I was in college, that was kind of the sound I had in my head, and it worked okay with Kenton, but it was really *too* dry. Finally, I went to a two-headed drum with a coated Ambassador on top and a clear one on the bottom, and I was very pleased when I did that. As you grow, you go through different stages of influence, and for some reason I got into the one-head thing for a while. I don't like the sound of a one-headed drum anymore. I associate it with that kind of "studio" sound. Single-head drums do have a certain unique sound, but I, myself, don't like that sound.

Then you have your single-head drums that come in fantastic shapes. Maybe for certain rock 'n' roll type things those drums are cool, but they're certainly not practical. They're too big to take on gigs. When you're a young, working drummer, you've got to work a lot of gigs. I worked a lot of dances, weddings, conventions, shows, and that kind of stuff. That's a pretty limited design for a drumset from a practical viewpoint.

You have companies like Yamaha, who's making a quality drum, and I think some of the other companies are trying to make good, honest drums. That's what the industry needs and should be doing. For the American drum makers, Drum Workshop is where I see hope. I'm only mentioning it because the quality of the drums really impressed me. I think the rest of the American drum companies will catch on and realize that they simply have to make a good, quality drum. No amount of holes they drill is going to make the drum any better. It's the quality of the wood and the roundness of the shell that matters. Take the hoop off and set the shell down on a glass table and see how it sits. If that drum sits perfectly flat, you know that a head has a fighting chance of sounding good on it. If it doesn't sit flat, well "caveat emptor." So look at how well the shell is made. That's what it comes down to. All the space-age materials and geometric shapes and holes drilled into the shell don't amount to anything without that basic quality being there. That's a very old-fashioned sounding kind of thing to say, but as I get older, I realize that's what drum-making should be about. I hope the American drum companies are going to start realizing this. The quality control in the American drums got a little shaky, and that's why the Japanese drums did so well. It just comes down to an instrument that sounds good and functions well. These gimmick things…

And the hardware—hopefully the "bigger is better" idea is being downplayed. I don't know what happened.

They were making cymbal stands that wouldn't even fit into a trap case. So what good does that do anybody? Except the endorsees who get all that shit free, and they have big, special cases for that stuff.

RM: And big roadies to carry it for them.

and I get them up there—and the stuff is sturdy. It just takes good design.

RM: A lot of people feel that loud music calls for big drums. Weather Report was loud, but you were using an 18" bass drum.

A&M Studios, 1978, during the recording of Joni Mitchell's "Mingus" album

Peter Erskine Library

PE: Even the big roadies don't like that stuff. I wonder what ever happened to the little flush-base cymbal stands. I hope they still make them. I always loved those little Ludwig and Slingerland flat-base stands. When I joined Kenton, that's what I had, and I was using huge cymbals. Like I said, my Yamaha hardware is not that big, but I can get the cymbal stands as high as I need them—

PE: At first, I had a 22" bass drum, with a hole in the front head and a little bit of padding. I got a good dry sound, it was easy for the sound man, and it worked well. But then I switched to an 18" and had it tuned up fairly tight. I remember the first rehearsal after I did that, we went through a tune and Wayne turned around, smiling, and said, "Definition! All *right*! Definition!" There was this

tone; the drum was speaking. If your drums have tone, they will cut through. If you're playing with a loud group, it generally means that the drums will be miked. A long time ago, Steve Gadd said in an article, "It's easier to get a good sound out of a small drum tuned looser than a large drum tightened up too much." Steve can get an amazingly huge drum sound, and his drums are not that big or that deep. So you don't need big drums. I mean, I like a beefy floor tom sometimes, and there's nothing that sounds like an 18" floor tom. But an 18" floor tom fills a pretty unique need, I think. If someone wants a set for a variety of things, they don't need drums that big. I currently use a 14" floor tom.

RM: When you first joined Weather Report, the group worked as a quartet for a while, and then Robert Thomas, Jr. joined on percussion. For you, what was the difference?

PE: Bobby made it a lot easier when he joined. The rhythm section before I joined was Alex [Acuna] and Manolo [Badrena], which I thought was the greatest. The album *Heavy Weather* came out, and I thought, "Wow! *This is* Weather Report. This is outasight!" By the time I joined, I think Zawinul wanted a little more clarity and not quite so much of a Latin angle on the thing. For a while, Joe grew kind of disaffected with all the shakers and things, so he opted for the quartet setting. Immediately, there was a lot more focus on the rest of the band. The drums provided a clearer pulse so that Joe, Wayne and Jaco could explore playing a little differently.

When Bobby came on, we had explored the quartet framework about as far as we were going to get. Bobby relieved me from having to go for a lot of different colors or filling in. I had started to branch out and do a little percussion. I had a little African balifon, some Synares, some tuned cowbells, and some gongs and stuff.

I was overplaying for a while with the group. I thought I always had to be filling in because Joe wanted to hear a lot of different things. He wanted to hear this beat going, but at the same time, he wanted to hear this other thing. It caused me to overplay for a while, because I was so worried about trying to do all these things I thought he wanted. Rhythmically, the key to Weather Report, I think, is that there's like two different time things going on. There's this one beat that's really propulsive and chugging ahead, and then the backbeat is like in half time. So we'd have this jazz thing with the cymbal, moving ahead, while the snare drum and bass drum were playing a half-time rock thing. It was a nice blend of contrasting rhythm things. It moves a certain way. When Bobby came in, it kind of enabled us to get closer to that idea. Bobby is a unique percussionist. He plays congas, bongos and cymbals all with his hands, so it is a different touch.

RM: One of the many unique things about that group was the fact that Jaco didn't function like a normal bass player.

PE: Yeah, he'd be all over the place. It was Jaco who heard me and got me into the group, more or less. I guess he heard something in my backbeat that he felt was strong enough so he would not have to do strict, traditional bass playing.

Jaco sometimes played the bass like a guitar, or he would start playing melodies. I'm working with Jaco now in his Word of Mouth group, and it's just bass, drums, percussionist, and two horns. The interesting thing is the openess of sound when the bass is not playing pure bass things. Somehow it reminds me of modern dance—the way the stuff moves around. It is different. Some drummers probably wouldn't enjoy playing with that kind of thing. They like more traditional bass playing, which I love too, but playing with Jaco has always been a treat for me. The thing with Jaco is, you can't get excited and just start thrashing around the drumset when he's doing something. See, anything in music needs a reference point. Weather Report stuff was getting out harmonically, and melodically it could be really strange, but there was a strong rhythmic reference point underneath—a cooking funk rhythm or something. If the stuff is getting spacy, there has to be some kind of reference point somewhere or else it's like chaos.

Certain free music is okay with chaos, but the best free music, if you really listen to it, has some very structured things to it. Any good free art—whether it be paintings, music or architecture—has a very strong sense of structure hidden somewhere in there. So that's the thing. If you're playing with a real creative musician, each of you, at certain points, has got to be respecting that sense of structure and keeping a basic reference point.

years ago. Joe and Jaco said, "If you ever play that way again, we'll kill you!" [laughs] They wanted me to always be composing, to be rhythmically creative, to never play unimaginatively, but not to play miscellaneously. It had to be clear, it had to be solid and strong—in other words, it had to be supportive. It's like the thing Zawinul said years ago about Weather Report: "We always solo and we never solo." And that's the way the drums had to be: always creative but never just bashing all over the place, or taking up too much musical space.

Maynard Ferguson and Peter performing at a gig

Peter Erskine Library

Not only for the listeners, but for the musicians as well. Otherwise, you're just rambling up there.

What I learned from Weather Report was not to get "miscellaneous" on the drums. One night, when I first joined the band, I got a little carried away. I was just filling in all over the place, much in the style of some drummers I used to listen to who were popular a few

RM: Why did you leave?

PE: I just thought it was time. I was in the group almost four years, and I wanted to come to New York and be a jazz musician and start exploring musical things a little bit more on my own. There are no burnt bridges or anything. I'll say this: I learned the most I've ever learned

about music and about life from working with that group—especially Joe Zawinul. I'm real happy that we finished that last record and got it out, because I think it shows really well how the band was playing and what point we'd reached conceptually. To me, Weather Report is a band about change, so it was time for something new, for them and for me. That's the fun. Weather Report is a musicians' band and people are always eager to see what they're going to do next. And you know it's always going to be good. So I look forward to seeing what they're going to come up with.

RM: Most young players, I think, dream of someday getting to play with "legendary" musicians. You were relatively young when you joined Weather Report. Were you ever awed by the fact that you were in a band with people like Joe Zawinul and Wayne Shorter?

PE: Sometimes it would strike me at odd times, like, "Wow, here I am shopping for post cards with *Wayne Shorter!*" But when you're actually playing, you just feel like one of the boys up there. You're right in the middle of it and you're doing it and it's great. There are times when you do sort of get outside yourself when you're playing. Things can get to the point where nothing can go wrong. You're not being self-conscious about your playing; you are, more or less, outside of yourself— kind of like you're out in the audience listening. Your ears are totally open to every thing. You hear everything that is happening because you are not worried about how you sound. And that moment is not something you can interrupt by thinking, "Geeze, here I am playing with *these guys!*" You feel incredible happiness that it sounds that good and that you're there doing it, but it's more of a Zen kind of thing.

RM: So, ideally, you concentrate on the music itself, rather than on what you are playing?

PE: It's like you know something so completely that you don't have to worry about technique or anything. There's nothing between the brain and the reflexes—the source of the action and the actual physical completion of the action. If you're listening to yourself, and you're auditing everything you're playing, you get these microsecond delays. Your time will start getting funny and creatively you choke up, instead of it all being very open.

It's like if you see another drummer walk into the club and you start worrying about how he thinks you sound, then you don't sound as good. If you don't know that anyone's there, you sound great. When you're relaxed and you are just listening to everything, you have less barriers. Your senses are totally responding to everything. It's an egoless kind of thing, and that's when you sound the best. That's when you kill 'em! That's when you *get down*, really *bad*.

RM: It can be stimulating for a musician to play with a lot of different people, in different situations. It can also be stimulating when certain musicians stay together year after year and grow together. Weather Report seemed to combine those two ideas: the group has been together for a long time, but they also take breaks during which the individual members can pursue other projects.

PE: Joe Zawinul encouraged me to play with a lot of other musicians, and play outside the group. I think it's good to play around with a lot of different things, and to hear something new and try to play it. The ability to play all kinds of music is great, but after a while, to satisfy your own sense of musical maturity, you have to build on something. You have to get your own sound together; your own tradition, of sorts; your own playing style.

I'd had visions of staying with Weather Report for years. I like the association of certain musicians that has gone on for years. I respect it, and I think it's very important because this age right now seems very transitory. People don't stick with anything—couples don't stick together, people get divorced like crazy; bands don't really stick together, there are always different groupings of musicians, and they work for a little while and then don't. To see some musicians have real commitments to each other—it's not just heartwarming, it's an inspiring kind of thing to see. I think it produces good musical results. Joe and Wayne, for example, are real partners, in the creative sense of the word. Weather Report, in that sense, wasn't a cooperative band. We were hired to play with them. But Steps is a cooperative group. We share. We make it or break it together. Really feeling a part of the musical, creative and financial success of something is an important incentive for a band to stick together.

It was great being in Weather Report. And yet, to leave the relative security of that to try and do something on my own seemed natural. To me, it didn't seem like any big deal. But it did, I guess, answer a need in me to find a little more of my own niche, evolving more towards the kind of player I want to be. My coming to New York was, in part, a desire to work with certain musicians—like the guys in Steps—and to find the musicians who I would like to explore music with for years to come. I feel that with Steps, I'm getting to play a lot of music that, for the first time, really sounds like me. It's a little closer to what I want to sound like and be perceived as, as a drummer.

RM: Wasn't Steps originally put together for Japan?

PE: Yeah. Originally, Steve Gadd was the drummer. Luckily, I got involved with the group at a certain point. For a while, it was just kind of a get-together thing where we had a good market in Japan and we would play in New York City. But then it got to the point of, "What are we going to do with our futures? Are we going to get serious or what? We have to know." We decided that we all liked the band enough to" make a commitment to it, so that Steps would be our first priority. If a Steps tour comes up, everything else has to be scheduled around that. That contributed to my ultimate decision to leave Weather Report. I'd made touring commitments with Steps for the summer, and after that, Weather Report decided to do a summer tour. You can't be in too many bands at once.

Steps has all the people who I love to play with. I think Michael Brecker is *the* musician of the '80s. His playing amazes me more every time I hear him. Mike Mainieri—I've been a fan of his since I was young. He's got the four-mallet thing totally together, but it's coming from a more soulful thing than a lot of four-mallet players. A lot of vibes players are into a more cerebral type thing; Mike *gets down!* And I'm getting an amazing experience playing with Eddie Gomez. I couldn't ask for anything more. Eddie has been the best thing to happen to me in terms of my time function. And Don Grolnick is a great piano player and composer. I'm learning a lot from him about different types of music.

The whole group is learning from each other. We have a lot of new music and we're still working on it, but there's a certain identity of sound already there. Our goal is to play the best improvisational music we can, whether it be in a Police-like rhythmic framework or it's bebop. The idea is that the songs be good compositions, and the compositions allow improvising. And there should be a certain spirit—there's just a certain jazz spirit or attitude we all have—that colors the sound. We're not trying to make something that will sell; we're just going to do it If by its own virtue it sells, I think that's the only way to do it.

"The ability to play all kinds of music is great, but after a while, to satisfy your own sense of musical maturity, you have to build on something."

RM: You recently did your first album under your own name for Contemporary Records. Were you happy with the way it came out?

PE: I am tremendously pleased with it. We did it in two days, and recorded everything, except for one tune, direct to two-track, so the audio quality and fidelity is outstanding. It's a live session—no overdubs—and everything was first or second takes, so the album is very fresh sounding. We did one tune multi-track where I overdubbed percussion and played a little bit of Oberheim synthesizer. And then in addition to the ensemble tunes, there is one little drum solo I played on there, just as a little signature. The drum sound we got is reminiscent of 1960s Blue Note jazz albums. It's not that real upfront kind of drum sound, but the blend is real good and you can hear everything real well. David Baker was the engineer and he did a very good job. I'm very happy with the balance and the texture of the sound.

I really couldn't be too much more pleased with it as a first representation under my own name. John Koenig, the producer, gave me the freedom to pick the material, the musicians and the concept of the album. I think it's the best playing I've done on record, and I'm also happy to have been able to present the other players in that kind of a setting. And I really loved getting to play with Don Alias on this album. He plays on every tune and he made everything completely smoking. Playing with him is a 100% treat. We play very well together.

RM: Did the two of you have to work things out in advance so you wouldn't get in each other's way?

PE: No, we didn't plan a thing. We are able to fall naturally into all sorts of different directions. Another amazing percussionist, who I've only played with a couple of nights, is Alex Acuña. You can put him on any instrument and he is a complete groove to play with. There are many great conga players around, but the guys who have excited me the most—Don and Alex—are both, interestingly enough, also drumset players.

RM: Have you ever done anything with them using two drumsets?

PE: No, but that would be interesting. When you're playing with musicians like those guys, they're so good you could be playing any instrument. Alex or Don could pick up a soda bottle and make it sound great. I've seen Zawinul do that. He could pick up the dumbest little toy instrument and make incredible music with it.

RM: I've seen Airto play a groove on a pack of cigarettes.

PE: Oh yeah, Airto is the king of that kind of stuff. That's what real music making is about: being able to make great music and create joy with anything. Just by clapping your hands and singing—that's the purest form. Then you start slapping your hands against something—bongos or whatever—and you're talking about some music.

RM: You wrote three of the tunes on the album. Was that your first experience with composing?

PE: I wrote some stuff in high school and college for theory class. I always opted to take composition classes because composing is very important. I hear a lot of music inside me but it's hard to get it out. When you begin composing, like I am now, you get a lot of vignettes—little portions that sound neat—but to expand on that you need more compositional technique. I'm going to have to start studying seriously. I usually set up a rhythm on my drum machine and then start improvising on the synthesizer. I don't have great keyboard facility or compositional technique, but improvising always brings out something original and creative. That gives me the germ for a new tune.

I can see why when songwriters write one tune they want to write more. It's intoxicating to hear your music played. The first time Steps played my "Coyote Blues," people told me, "You looked like the father of a newborn baby." Just hearing it was such a kick. Of course, with musicians like that, you don't have to write too much and they bring it to life. They bring the humble little notes you have on paper to sounding like some real music.

So I recommend to all drummers to study keyboard. Even if piano lessons aren't fun, don't give it up. Take keyboard, learn theory, learn harmony, and compose. Don't just dip your toes in the water—jump in and start doing it.

RM: A lot of drummers can't compose because they don't know enough about music.

PE: You've got the same responsibility to know as much about the music as any other musician. I mean, drums are initially easier to play than a violin or clarinet. You just walk up and hit a drum and it makes a sound. With a clarinet, it can take a week just to get a squeak. But after a point, the artistic demand is equally as high on all instruments. Even to get a perfect sound out of a triangle takes true artistry. The percussionists in the New York Philharmonic are as great musicians as anyone else in that orchestra. And I couldn't conceive of thinking of Elvin Jones in terms any less than Coltrane.

A drummer has to know music and song forms and so on. When you're playing with a band and they say "Take it," you've got to be able to play on the tune form—whether it's a 12-bar blues, a standard, or whatever—and play a musical solo. If you know the melody and harmony, that will all come out in your drumming. When people say that someone is a "musical drummer," it's because the drummer plays with harmonic and melodic sense. Max Roach is a great example of someone who plays musically on the drumset, and he knows all of the mallet instruments and he composes. That's what it takes.

Guys like Michael Brecker, who's a horn player, and Jaco, who plays bass—these guys can sit down at my drumset and sound great. They've all got their own beats. All of the horn players who have played with Elvin can play mean drums. It's important for them to know about the drums, and it's important for a drummer to know about the things that make up the rest of the music world. After a show, Joe and Jaco would sometimes talk about something they had played like it was an inside joke. They would say things like, "... and when you went into that E-flat and I played...," and they would be laughing with glee because one guy played *this* substitution on top of *that*. You've got to learn the language. You're in for a lot more fun. I have some books Dan Haerle wrote for keyboard, and I'm eating them up, learning about voicings. I know a good voicing when I hear one, but when I look at the

Peter playing his Ludwig drumset and big Zildjian cymbals with Stan Kenton, 1972

keyboard, I can't extract one as quickly as I want to.

I wish I'd taken my piano lessons more seriously. I used to go, "Yuk! I hate it!" I used to make up excuses to cancel my piano lesson because I hadn't practiced. You know, you can only do so much when you're a kid and still remain a kid. But the good music schools require a certain keyboard proficiency. Most people get through it and then forget about it, but the intent behind it is good. Look at Jack DeJohnette—I think he originally was a piano player. I've heard him play piano on gigs. It's wild.

RM: Philly Joe plays piano too, and Elvin plays guitar.
PE: Yeah? He plays guitar? I didn't know that!

RM: Check out "Elvin's Guitar Blues" on the *Heavy Sounds* album.

PE: That's it. That's why *he* plays so melodically. He knows the stuff.

RM: Do you ever feel that too many drummers are just concerned with chops, rather than with music?

PE: I don't know. That was always the picture. It's amazingly seductive to go wild on the drums because it feels so good, and a lot of us go through periods of overplaying the instrument. And there's the whole thing of the glorified drum solo where people go crazy. People like that. People like to watch a building burning down and people like to see a drummer go crazy during a drum solo. But a musician has to think, "What am I doing with this instrument here? What do I want to say?" I think when you're younger, you go for that flashier kind of thing because you get that feedback of "Wow!" when you're doing a big-deal drum solo and sweat is flying and you're having a heart attack by the end of the thing. But after a while you prove to yourself that you can play that stuff, and getting "Wows!" from the audience becomes less and less important. It's good to play with some energy, and I think it's good to blend a little bit of drama into your music. You want to get your audience into what you're doing. But as far as long drum solos and stuff, I think you should ask yourself, "Musically, is that really what's happening?" A lot of musicians aren't really crazy about a lot of drum solos. I think the trend is more towards musicality.

When I hear a drummer, I listen for the propulsion of the time, the smoothness, the clarity of the rhythms, and if it just feels good. When I hear great drummers, I find myself laughing. It's so much fun to hear someone do something well. My mouth can drop open at what some drummers do, but I don't find myself really feeling good that I heard it, as opposed to the way I feel when I hear one of the real masters. I listen to bebop drummers a lot for inspiration. I think that's a good thing to check out if you want to play any jazz at all, because these drummers are geniuses—the musicality and sense of humor they have; the way the stuff swings; the way it moves. I want to get closer to the way Elvin Jones plays—the way the sound just rolls out and propels everything.

Listening to some of the more contemporary classical music has been a real good influence because of the way some composers do the variations of themes, and the way they compress and expand the themes. I try to do that when I compose at the drums. When I play a solo, I try to keep it thematic. To me, whatever you play has to continue what has gone on before and move towards what will go on after. It has to make some kind of musical sense. It's not just going wild. It's like telling a good joke—it has to build to something. But some comedians get laughs just by running around and falling down a lot.

RM: I've spoken to some musicians who have very definite ideas about where they fit in historically with what they are doing. Do you ever look at yourself in that way?

PE: Not really. I have a pretty good sense of self, in that I know what I can do, what I can't do, and what I want to do. After playing with Weather Report, I discovered that there are a lot of things I want to learn, but one thing I *do* know is, after playing with them, I'm not afraid to play with anyone. I feel strong as a musician, and I feel confident in my ability to play the drums, and I'm glad for that. You can't sit around and worry about how people are going to judge you historically, because then you will be living in some kind of future tense. It's a very ego-oriented trip. It's like thinking, "When I'm dead, everybody's really going to miss me."

I feel a comfortable synthesis of what I play. I'm a product of our nuclear age. I would love to be coming from a more jazz direction, but I love playing all sorts of stuff. So I just hope I can continue playing with good musicians for the rest of my life, because I really don't enjoy much else. I don't have too many hobbies. I guess I'm not the well-rounded genius I always hoped I would be. [laughs] Athletically, I'm a disgrace. If *Modern Drummer* puts together a softball team, don't bother calling me for it. I've got to get that a little more together, because sports are a good thing for musicians to be in. It keeps you vital. You can't just be a musician. You've got to get out in the world.

RM: That idea of a musician needing to get out in the world brings up something you said earlier about learning a lot about life while you were in Weather Report. How does life experience affect one's musicianship?

PE: I think the most vital music is created by musicians who are vital people. They have something to offer. Music is only a reflection. Once you get past the things you learned in school—the techniques and licks and whatever—it's what you are and what you believe in that's going to come out. Sometimes that's a subtle influence and sometimes it's pretty profound. Certainly in drumming it's very evident. You can hear from the music what kind of person that drummer is. The amount of space, the sensitivity which involves shadings and touch, the way the music is propelled, how hard it swings or how gutsy it is—that's all reflective of a drummer's personality. The reason a person plays a certain way is because something inside the person picks up on something and uses that in the music.

RM: Do you ever consciously call on some experience or emotion while you're playing?

PE: No. Sometimes that inadvertently happens. You might flash on something, but that's very rare. Only a couple of times have I been playing my instrument where at the same point I got very upset about something and maybe started hitting the drums harder. Drums are a nice physical release, and that release can be good. Sometimes in Weather Report, Joe would try to provoke certain outbursts from me on the drums to sort of let me experience the freedom that comes. But even if you get real angry on your instrument, you have to control and discipline your anger. You can't just go apeshit and start banging away at everything. You have to channel that anger into a statement. So I don't consciously call on things, like "method" music making. It just seems to come out.

There's also a certain amount of artistic integrity and professionalism involved. Just because you've had a lousy day you don't go out and make your audience feel uncomfortable. I mean, you've got to realize that people pay money to come and hear you. So you've got to do the best you can under the circumstances. It's hard to separate, but yet, a lot of times I've played my best when I've really felt sick. I've had the flu or something, and the last thing I'm worried about is how I sound—I just want to get through it. When that happens, you often play very well because you're not self-conscious about how you sound. You're functioning on a real musical level. The final thing it comes down to is, how does it sound? When you're talking about being a professional musician, that's all that matters. Not every night is going to be the best, but you *try* your best and see what you get.

"I think the most vital music is created by musicians who are vital people. They have something to offer."

Peter Erskine
1987 On The Cover

By Rick Mattingly

Peter Erskine is laughing. "Steve Khan just called," he tells me. "He's joining Weather Update, and the band is meeting in Vienna next week to rehearse for the European tour. Steve wanted to know if he and I could get together sometime this week to run through a few things so that he 'll be prepared for the first rehearsal. I told him, 'No way, pal! You'll have to join this band the same way the rest of us did.'"

Several months later, I reminded Peter of that incident, and asked him if one could, perhaps, accuse him of being… well, coldhearted towards a fellow musician? Peter chuckles at the memory, looking slightly sheepish for a moment. But then he laughs it off "Nah, it wasn't coldhearted. That was just my way of telling Steve that he was great enough to go in there and play without preparing anything. If you just plop yourself into a situation, the chemical reaction will be more interesting than if you prepare the ingredients beforehand and then let them set for a while." Peter should know. In 1981, after living in California for several years, he "plopped" himself into New York City in the hopes of making a living playing jazz. Granted, he came to town with some impressive credentials: Stan Kenton, Maynard Ferguson, Weather Report. But that doesn't guarantee anything in a town like New York, where there are plenty of musicians with equally impressive credits who are not working regularly. But within a relatively short period of time, Peter was turning up with increasing frequency in various New York jazz clubs, and he was invited to replace Steve Gadd in the group Steps Ahead.

For a couple of years, that group was Peter's main focus. But as the members got more involved in technology and less involved in mainstream jazz, the group's identity seemed to suffer (like when they got involved in doing the music for a Jane Fonda exercise record). Personnel started changing, and the group was having trouble completing its third album. Erskine, meanwhile, was on a creative roll. In 1986 alone, he performed and recorded with John Abercrombie, with the group Bass Desires, wrote a drum book, and composed the incidental music for a production of Richard II. Then, as things with Steps Ahead seemed to be falling apart, he was invited to record with Weather Report and to rejoin the group for the subsequent tour.

As it turned out, that was probably the last Weather Report album, as Wayne Shorter left the group after the record came out. For the tour, the group was renamed Weather Update, but whether that marks the beginning of something new or merely the end of an era remains to be seen.

For Peter Erskine, however, it was the beginning of a transition period that represented a number of things coming full circle for him. When he'd first joined Weather Report, he was the protege under the wings of Joe Zawinul, Wayne Shorter, and Jaco Pastorius. Moving to New York could be viewed as leaving the nest, and with Steps Ahead, he learned to fly on his own. When he returned to Weather Report, his input was on such a high level that Zawinul invited Peter to co-produce the album.

And now, as we sit in Peter's New York apartment to do this interview, we are surrounded by packing boxes, which represent another full circle in Peter's life: He's moving back to California. The reason is personal rather than musical; Peter is about to become a father, and he feels that California is a better place to raise a family than the streets of New York.

As far as I'm concerned, it's New York's loss and California's gain, because Peter has a vitality and energy that rub off on the people around him. I've spent a lot of time with Peter over the past few years, and somehow, I always come away feeling inspired. In fact, on a couple of occasions when I've felt somewhat burned out, I've purposely sought out Peter's company, knowing that his positive energy would stimulate me. And it's not just some kind of Pollyanna happy attitude; Peter questions, analyzes, challenges, he thinks.

That's evident in this interview. With all of the changes going on in his life, Peter is in a reflective mood. So we examine some things from the past, but mostly we look ahead to what these things will mean for the future, because Peter is, as always, moving ahead.

RM: You seem to enjoy living dangerously. When Weather Update toured America last summer, you used the new Yamaha electronic drums, which you had just gotten the day before the tour started. If something had gone wrong, you would have been stuck.

PE: Yeah, I had never played a totally electronic kit in a band before. I'd used a couple of pads here and there, along with a regular drumkit. But my initial interest in electronics had to do with triggering sounds from the acoustic drums. I enjoyed being able to kick in an electronic sound at a certain point that could make a floor tom sound like the end of the world. If you've got a good sound system, something like that can be very effective, if you use it judiciously. So I had a Simmons SDS5, which was perfect for that. It had a fat, beefy, analog sound.

I first heard the Yamaha system when some of the Yamaha people brought one to S. I. R. in New York. They invited a bunch of drummers to come in, play it, and make suggestions. One of the guys had a note pad, and he was taking down all of the comments.

RM: As I recall, he actually had a portable computer.

PE: Oh, yeah. That shows you how times are changing. Anyway, as soon as I heard those sounds, I realized that I didn't want to have to hear a drum when all I wanted was a clave. So, all of a sudden, triggering sounds from acoustic drums didn't seem to be the answer anymore.

Also, around that same time I was dealing with the problems and frustrations of miking, because whenever you're miking acoustic instruments, you run into problems with mic's being out of phase with each other and with leakage. In other words, you can throw a microphone in front of a snare drum and get a great snare drum sound, but if you've got another mic on your tom-tom, then that mic' picks up a little snare drum, and the snare drum mic' picks up a little tom-tom. By the time you add a whole kit's worth of

"I enjoyed being able to kick in an electronic sound at a certain point that could make a floor tom sound like the end of the world."

microphones, that great snare drum sound has changed.

In a room where you're not using a P.A. system, the natural acoustic sound is the best. But when you're going through a P.A., the drums have to sound good coming through the speakers. The instrument has changed. It's not purely an acoustic instrument anymore; the microphone is the interface, and you're now dealing with electronics.

So if you're dealing with electronics anyway, you are going to get a better sound by using pure electronics than by using a combination of acoustics and electronics. You can get a pure tom-tom sound without getting cymbal wash or leakage from other drums. And you can still retain the nature of live performance. It's not like you're using a machine instead of a person. I'm still playing. And with the Yamaha system, I can access hundreds of sounds quickly. If I want a perfectly mic'ed clave sound, I can get it by hitting a pad. I don't have to put down my sticks to pick up a pair of claves, and I don't hear a tom sound like I would if I were triggering the clave sound from an acoustic drum. And then I can hit a button and get a cowbell sound, or a steel drum, or whatever I want. I would need a table 20 feet long to hold all of those instruments, and then I'd be going crazy trying to reach them all. So for someone interested in percussion sounds for live work, this is the answer.

RM: Did you have to adjust your technique in any way?

PE: A little. Playing on the pads is different than playing on an acoustic drum. The dynamic range is a little bit different. When you hit the pad, the sound doesn't come from the point of contact but from wherever your speaker is placed. That's a big difference.

What I liked was that it made me think carefully about orchestration. Sometimes, when I'm playing a beat, I get it to lay a certain way by filling it out on other parts of the kit, like maybe some little tom-tom notes. But a lot of electronic sounds take up more sonic room than acoustic sounds. So if I've got a big electronic tom sound instead of a nice, centered little 13" tom, I've got to be more careful with where I place that note because it's taking up so much room. I find that it imposes a good discipline on me. I'm playing much clearer and more concisely, and thus using the sounds to greater effect.

RM: I started out by accusing you of living dangerously by taking a setup on the road that you weren't used to. But I can also see a positive side to that, in terms of giving yourself a new challenge to keep yourself on your toes. I'm reminded of Elvin once saying that he sometimes switches his cymbals around so he'll have to think about where a particular sound is, and because it helps keep him from just doing the same things out of habit.

PE: That's a very good point. That's why I change actual cymbals sometimes. Recently I was recording with Makoto Ozone, and my cartage guy brought the wrong floor tom. I had my little 18" bass drum, a real crisp snare, a small tom with an Ambassador that was cranked way up high, and this huge floor tom with a clear Emperor tuned real low. There was this huge spread between the small tom and the floor tom, but the bass drum and floor tom together sounded like timpani. It changed the way I played a little bit, because certain things that I would have done on a smaller floor tom wouldn't have worked on this one. But it was a fun challenge. Gary Burton was producing, and he came over and said, "You know, that was interesting. When you first played the individual toms, they sounded so different. But the way you used them made the kit sound like a complete whole."

Electronic drums can have the same effect. Using them changes the way you play so that you don't rely on the same things. Some drummers have a sound that works for them, and it's always the same. But sometimes when they're playing with different people, they should be coming up with different stuff.

Unfortunately, they kind of sound the same on every record. Maybe that's what they're hired to do, but I like changing the venue, so to speak.

RM: In the interview we did four years ago, you were telling me about going to the NAMM show. Before you went, you were really excited about seeing some of the new electronic instruments, but when you actually got there, the thing that still grabbed you the most was the sound of really great acoustic instruments. What's changed? Have electronics improved a lot since then, or have you decided that something has to be sacrificed to meet the current needs?

PE: No, they're two different things. My greatest pleasure still comes from sitting down behind a four-piece acoustic kit. Physically, it's a very intimate setup. No wires- I can play by candlelight if I have to. [laughs] On the Weather Update tour, in addition to the complete electronic kit, I had an 8 x 14 acoustic snare drum, a 22 x 16 acoustic bass drum, and real cymbals. I still need a real snare drum, hihat, and cymbals, and I like to have a real bass drum. With those instruments, I have a complete dynamic range for the nuances I want. I can't imagine sitting down at a complete electronic kit without a couple of real drums and cymbals. Maybe, deep down, I'm just a bebopper at heart.

At the same time, electronics certainly have

Peter 1972

Clark Chaffee/Peter Erskine Library

improved. They've permeated society and are here to stay. There's going to be a lot of great music played on electronic instruments, as well as a lot of stinko music- just like there's good music and crappy music played on acoustic instruments. I think that people are getting a little weary of listening to stuff that's overly sequenced. You see less and less drum machines at recording sessions and more and more drummers. So everything does go in cycles. Acoustic instruments are still the greatest to play. But electronics are the door to the future-to endless possibilities.

If you want to concentrate on the acoustic drum set and use your energy to develop that to its greatest potential, that's terrific. But other people realize that the world's a big place, and they want to get into some other stuff. Emil Richards, for example, has one of the most extensive percussion collections in the world, and he's using electronics to preserve that collection. He's sampling his instruments, and that's going to save them from the wear and tear of being moved around to various studios and being used on soundtracks and recordings. In a lot of cases, a digitally sampled version of an instrument will suffice.

So getting back to your question about what has changed in the last few years, electronics have definitely improved-specifically in the area of percussion. They're on par now with keyboard instruments, and you couldn't say that four years ago. Most of the stuff that was out then isn't even available anymore, but they were the necessary building blocks. In the manual for Total Music software, which is what I use on my Macintosh, there's a great quote: "Pioneers are the guys with the arrows in their backs." So we owe many thanks to the people who put a lot on the line and envisioned those first electronic drums. But better instruments have now come along. That's the way electronics is, whether it's computers or instruments.

RM: One thing that bothers some people about electronics is that a lot of current music seems to be just sounds rather than composition.

PE: Well, what is composition? What is music? What makes a piece of art interesting? Artists tend to feel that, if it produces some kind of reaction, then it's good. If people don't react, that's awful. Of course, most of us would like it to be a good reaction, because our egos are involved. So anyway, it comes down to personal aesthetics. For the person who came up with those sounds, it may be very meaningful, and there may be a lot of people who enjoy it. A lot of people really dig Barry Manilow. Personally, I don't turn to him for any kind of inspiration; in fact, I avoid him. That's just my taste. It's like, "A hundred thousand Barry Manilow fans can't be wrong." As far as I'm concerned, they can, but as far as they're concerned, they're not. So what's the answer?

RM: The reason I asked the question was because I feel that a good composition should not have to depend on a particular set of sounds. For example, think of the Weather Report tune "Birdland." I love the original recording of that, and the way that Joe Zawinul combined synthesizer and acoustic piano was truly inspired. But the tune also works with the Manhattan Transfer singing all of the parts. So the composition works by itself.

PE: That's a valid point. Joe is a masterful composer. Because of his musical knowledge and his hipness or whatever, he creates music that has a great sense of structure. Beethoven's "Fifth Symphony" was transcribed for piano, and it sounds good. The composition stands up. But it sounds better with an orchestra, because that is what it was conceived for. The orchestration is important. There's a reason that the violins are playing a certain section rather than 14 bassoons.

RM: Okay, that's a valid point, too. I guess what I object to is just pushing button after button to get a variety of sounds and calling that creativity. Finding the right sound can be creative, and yet…

PE: Yeah. A synthesizer comes with a lot of programs built in, and you can just sit there like a monkey pushing all of the buttons. "Wow, listen to this! It's a spaceship taking off!" A synth may only have a couple of really usable sounds. Some musicians get involved in programming their own sounds. Some don't. Some say that they don't want to be programmers; they want to be musicians. So they pick a synth that has usable sounds.

When you were talking about the person pushing button after button, the first image that came into my mind was the situation we've arrived at, particularly in this country, where someone will sit in front of a TV with a cable and remote control, and just switch channels endlessly. It becomes a mishmash of programs and commercials, a

1969 Peter on his new Ludwig drumset

F.A. Erskine, M.D.

wasteland. Maybe there's some kind of parallel there, like a person with a synth who has all of these sounds, but who never truly gets involved with what each sound will do. My Yamaha electronic system can produce all sorts of sounds, but when I used it on my solo album, I was only dealing with three different kit sounds. It's like with an acoustic setup. You tune your drums a certain way and you pick a certain set of cymbals, and then you make the most of those sounds.

This brings up something that we talked about after you heard the last Steps Ahead record. You said that you couldn't tell who was playing what. Mike Mainieri has always been my favorite vibes player because of his touch on the instrument. His sound on the vibes gave Steps a uniqueness. But now he just sounds like a DX7. Yes, it's still his phrasing and ideas, but I think you can lose a certain amount of the player's identity if there's too much MIDI-thru going on. I don't think a lot of people would be interested in hearing Horowitz play an electric piano.

Going back to that television analogy, the typical vision of modern man is someone eating dinner and watching a report of this many people dying, and then boom, switch over to Wheel Of Fortune. The end result is that nothing really means anything. Maybe that's true of a lot of our music: Nothing means anything. What kind of involvement or dedication do people have to their instruments? What kind of discipline is involved? I always think of a craftsman who has dedicated his life to, say, working with wood. He doesn't have the TV or radio on when he's working, and he's concentrating completely on what he's doing. He makes something that he's very proud of, because it represents all that he can be.

I think that's why a lot of us got into music, that sense of accomplishment and pride. And it's exciting to work with other musicians and feel, "Wow, we did it!" It's that comradery of being in an ensemble, looking at each other, smiling, and saying, "That really sounded good." It's even better than, "Look what I did." You get the added benefit of, "Look what we did." All the buttons in the world aren't going to do that for you. Sure, you can sit in your basement with sequencers and drum machines, and multi-track yourself all over the place. But the real joy of music making is those moments of spontaneity, of interaction, of chance taking-not programming a drum machine to play this and sequencing something to go with that. Big deal. Bruce Springsteen and his band can play for four hours and keep thousands of people excited, because they have energy. Who's going to want to sit around and watch someone push buttons for four hours?

There's always going to be good art and bad art. Whether you restrict people to a pencil or give them a Macintosh, some people will have something valid to put on the paper and some won't. But if someone uses the computer to print junk, you can't indict the computer for that. You can't indict synthesizers for bad music. I think people are going to accomplish great things with electronics. We're just scratching the surface with this stuff, and there's a whole lot more that people are going to be able to do. It represents a pretty big upheaval in terms of technology, and it's already had a big effect. But you've got to remember that, when phonograph records first came out, a lot of people thought that was the end of live performance. It wasn't. It actually created more demand for live performance because it exposed more people to music. So right now, we're just experiencing some growing pains of the information age, I guess.

RM: Do you ever feel that you're spending too much time reading manuals instead of playing?

PE: No, I like it. [laughs] I wish there were more hours in the day. When I see what other drummers are doing, then I want to know about it. Now that I'm moving to Los Angeles, I'm going to have to get my electronics

A young Peter playing while his drum teacher, John Civera looks on. Note Peter's father's hand holding the bottom of the bass drum so that it doesn't move.

Peter Erskine Library

into that state-of-the-art standard that they have out there. All the drummers have racks the size of deep freezers. It's almost out of control, but someone set the standard, and everyone else has to come up to that to be considered on par. It's kind of competitive overkill.

I think the ultimate question we're getting at here is: Will the mist clear, and will some musicians find a path, pursue it, and find some part of their true musical selves? Or do these instruments represent another aspect of consumer society running amuck?

RM: I know that you are a consumer junkie ....

PE: You should see my MasterCard statement. A few of us are going to start a group called "D.A." (Digital Anonymous.) We'll have meetings where people will stand up and say, "MIDI has made my life completely unmanageable."

RM: You've got an apartment full of electronics, but I also know that, as much as you enjoy fooling around with that stuff, it doesn't compare with your excitement when you find a great cymbal or when you have a really great experience within a band.

PE: It's true. All of the electronic stuff is the hobby. The drum set is my craft, my life's work. At the same time, the synthesizers and the Macintosh have helped me compose music and write a drum book. I'm actually using this stuff to realize my goals; it's not just sitting in the closet. I'm not much of a keyboard player at all, but I've got a bunch of synths, and the Total Music software lets me enter stuff on the Mac at my own speed. And with the new Yamaha system, I can now access MIDI through drum pads. Performance wise as well as compositionally, the horizon is really teeming with possibilities.

RM: Just a couple of years ago, it seemed that technology was working against drummers, when you consider how many drummers lost work because of drum machines. But now it seems that technology has caught up with drummers, and there are some new opportunities opening. Through MIDI, drummers are getting the chance to show that they have musical ideas that are perfectly valid.

PE: Yeah. The realities have changed for a lot of musicians. I don't think that most people are abandoning everything they've ever cherished just to grab onto the electronic thing. Electronics are potentially capable of great things. It's still in its infant stage, and I think that the excitement and preoccupation with the whole thing just reflects its youth.

I just realized that I'm probably contradicting myself. A little while ago, I said that this stuff is a reflection of consumer society running amuck, and I still stand by what I said in the last interview about how I'd rather hear Elvin hit a drum than hear anybody push a button. At the same time, it depends on who's pushing the button and what's on the disk. The point is, one doesn't exclude the other. If you can use electronics to do your thing, great.

RM: I certainly enjoyed the way that you used the Yamaha system to get that steel drum sound on your new solo album. I was wishing that the piece had gone on a little longer.

PE: That was just a little thing I wrote one night in a hotel room in Philly. I had only played two shows with the new system, and we had a day off. I took the kit up to my hotel room because I was still trying to learn how to use the system. One of the things you can program into the PMCI is Dynamic Note Shift, which means that when you strike the pad harder you get a different note. You can have up to five different notes on each pad. So I got a steel drum sound, and then programmed a pentatonic scale, so that even if I goofed and hit a pad a little too hard, I would still get a note that worked. So I had that programmed into MIDI A, and then on MIDI B, I had sampled conga drums from the Korg DDD-1. They were playing in harmony with the steel drum sounds.

That piece started out as an improvisation. At some point in my solo on the Weather Update tour, I would use that sound, and it gradually evolved into a short piece.

Charlie Haden, Peter, Akiko Yano and Pat Metheny taken during a recordfing session for her album "Welcome Back" recorded at the Power Station in New York, circa 1989

RM: The record also contains some music from *Richard III*. Is that the exact music that you wrote for the play, or is this just based on that?

PE: The orchestral sounding stuff (the French horn pieces) was used that way in the production. The two jazz pieces were just based on those themes. It wasn't like the score was "Jazz Meets Shakespeare." But I liked a couple of the melodies and thought that they would work well as jazz tunes.

RM: The way this album is mixed, I was suddenly aware of how much you like to hit crash cymbals. I had never really noticed that before, but then I went back and listened to some other records that you're on, and I realized that hitting a lot of cymbal crashes is something that you do pretty consistently.

PE: The main two colors on the cymbal are the dry, short tone that you get with the tip of the stick and the broad spread of a crash. Crashes are a very warm way of marking time or spreading the beat. Also, the neat thing about recording with crashes is that you can use stereo imaging to move the sounds around from right to left. If you get a couple of nice crashes relatively off mic', it's kind of interesting, it's not just "ting, ting, ting" all of the time.

One thing that I like to do is hit crashes without hitting the bass drum or snare drum. Someone pointed out to me that Shelly Manne used to do that, too. In other words, a lot of drummers always hit a drum along with a crash cymbal, which makes it like an exclamation point. But I like to hit cymbals by themselves.

RM: A few years ago, you had your cymbals positioned at rather extreme angles. But now your cymbals are positioned horizontally. Did the angle change gradually or all of a sudden?

PE: It was kind of gradual. The Zildjian people were always telling me that my cymbals would sound better if I leveled them out. If you want a cymbal to sound the way that it really sounds, it should be horizontal and not clamped down. At one time, I thought that having the cymbals at that angle gave me a certain stick to cymbal attitude. I thought that was a good setup for me. It wasn't. That gave me some real problems with my playing. I just wasn't making good contact with the instrument. There was an actual time lag in getting from the drums up to the cymbals and down again. When you're playing drums, if you can play very relaxed and efficiently, then your ideas have a much better chance of coming out.

I once sat in on a guy's set in Chicago, and he had everything very flat. When I played on his drums, I thought, "What a neat idea." But it took a few years for that to sink in. Now I see pictures of myself from a few years ago, and when I see the way those cymbals are tilted, I think, "That's really not good."

RM: With a lot of drummers, even though they may be multifaceted, there's usually a characteristic that comes to mind when the person's name is mentioned. For instance, if someone mentioned Steve Jordan, you might think of ...

PE: Backbeat-the world's greatest.

RM: Danny Gottlieb's name might make someone think of cymbals. With Mel Lewis, I always think of the way he supports. What about Peter Erskine? How would you define yourself?

PE: If I had to think of something that makes me unique-besides the fact that my family might find me endearing-then I think that it would be that I've got a pretty good backbeat and I can also swing, and at the same time, I can play music that's open in terms of form.

I was thinking recently that a lot of the music I play simply involves listening to the other musicians, because I can't go in with any preconceived ideas of how it's going to be. For example, I just did an ECM record with Gary Peacock, who plays bass a little more on top of the beat than what I'm used to. He also plays around the beat a lot; you don't get a lot of downbeats. On the first take, I had trouble following him. I wasn't exactly trusting what he was playing. But as I listened to the playback, I could hear exactly what he was doing. The way he was developing around the motion of the music was ingenious. Then [producer] Manfred Eicher came over to me and said, "Listen. Just listen." When we played it again, I just listened to Gary, without worrying about the beat. The musicians all had enough experience to supply the beat for themselves. So this was one of the first times that I've played something where the time wasn't being played, but it was always there. It turned out to be an extraordinary take. I was thrilled. It's the kind of stuff I've heard Paul Motian play.

As far as drumming goes, I've realized that you can't be everything to everybody. For better or worse, after a while, you arrive at a way of playing. You can try to improve that, but you can't change who you are. You can be influenced by Elvin or Tony or Gadd or Porcaro or Weckl or whoever, but you can't try to be that person. When you hear somebody doing something great, it's natural to say, "I want some of that in my playing," and your ego wants you to be highly regarded in a lot of areas. But you've got to do what you can do.

I think of myself as a jazz drummer. The people in L.A. seem to think of me that way. I've already had a couple of people say, "You're a jazz drummer. Are you sure you want to come out here?" To some hardcore be-boppers, I'm not a jazz drummer, I'm a fusion drummer.

Basically, I play the music I play because it's the music I enjoy. I recognize certain obligations to tradition and to taste, but the primary motivating factor for most artists, I think, is to satisfy themselves.

Some people get on a high horse and say things like, "I'm here to ensure that the tradition of jazz continues." Okay, maybe they feel a sense of responsibility, but the real reason they're playing it is because they dig it. And when you dig something, you play it convincingly. That's why jazz played by jazz musicians sounds good, or why rock 'n' roll played by rock musicians sounds good. The people who are playing it believe in it, so the music rings true.

I'm real happy about a recent batch of recordings that I've done for Denon: my own solo album, *Transition*; an Eliane Elias album with Eddie Gomez; and Bob Berg's recording with Don Grolnick, Will Lee, and Mike Stern. These three recordings document the different facets of my playing. For example, I love playing with acoustic bass players like Eddie and Marc Johnson, and I also love working with electric bass players like Will Lee, who's my favorite. On these three recordings, I got to play with all three of those guys.

Capitol Studios with Joel McNeely conducting a Seth MacFarlane session.

Peter Erskine Library

RM: If I had to describe your drumming in one word,

the word I'd use would be "protagonist." You don't just sit in the back and react to everyone else. You are also throwing out ideas of your own, and I often get the sense that you are pushing the other musicians to greater heights.

PE: That's a nice compliment. Recently, I was reading reviews of some albums I've played on, and they were saying things like, "The support was tasteful." I guess that's nice, but . . . After one of the takes on the ECM record, I was just talking about, Jan Garbarek came up to me and said, "Very good. You took charge." When I first started playing free music, I was always just responding to what somebody else did. I feel more comfortable now, and if I feel like making a statement, I do. I also try to be supportive.

The nice thing is that I feel like I can do more without the ego being involved. Before, I felt that I had to leave a thumbprint, so I would do something goofy on almost every take just because I thought I was branding it as being me. It was a kind of conceit. The only thing it got branded as was being goofy. It used to drive Mike Mainieri crazy. "Why did you do that?" He had a good point a lot of times. So now maybe I've got a slightly more mature way of interacting.

RM: One record on which I especially got that feeling of you being a protagonist was the Bass Desires album. I got a real sense that all of the musicians were contributing equally.

PE: That's what coming to New York did for me. That music demands that kind of involvement or interaction. Also, musicians like Marc Johnson, Bill Frisell, and John Scofield play with the right amount of space that allows that. I do enjoy playing with musicians who leave room for stuff to happen.

RM: Another thing I noticed on that album had to do with the relationship between your ride cymbal and the drums. With a lot of drummers, it seems as if everything is sort of based around the ride cymbal time. In fact, on some of your older recordings, that was the feeling I had. But on more recent stuff, there seems to be more interplay with the whole kit.

PE: I think I feel more comfortable playing drums now, and I don't need to always keep the time going "ding, ding, ding" on the ride cymbal. I did for a long time. When you first start out, it's real important to develop that concept of keeping time on the cymbal. But eventually you can internalize that feeling, that knowledge, so that you can then not play it and the time will still be there.

For example, last night I was recording with Eliane Elias, and when we did the first take, I started playing "ding ding a ding." But that seemed too crowded with what the piano and bass were doing, so the next time we played it, I just played one cymbal note per bar. The time was happening in other parts of the group, so it wasn't necessary for me to play "ding ding a ding." The style of music didn't require me to play that. If it had been Dixieland, I would have had to play that style, or if it had been bebop, there would have been certain stylistic things needed. But a lot of the music that I seem to be playing now doesn't require that I do that. But the time is still happening within me and, hopefully, within the other musicians.

RM: On that same album, there's a tune called "Mojo Highway" that has an interesting beat. You seem to be playing a combination of funk, shuffle, and reggae.

PE: That's all music that I like. I think you can tell who a drummer has listened to. Some people put different things together, and it comes out sounding unique. With someone like Dave Weckl, you can tell that he's spent a lot of time listening to backbeat and in-the-pocket stuff. Jeff Watts seems to have an interesting combination of people he's listened to.

Of course, there are also some drummers who have a technical proficiency that reflects more practice hours than musical hours. I'm not saying that it's not musical necessarily, but I just don't hear the years of experience. I may be getting myself into a funny corner here.

Peter Erskine Library

RM: Well, since you brought up practicing, I was wondering about a tune on the Weather Report *This Is This* album. On the tune "Update" the tempo is really fast. I don't know you to be someone who sits down and practices regularly, so how do you come up with the chops to play that fast?

PE: I've gotten grilled by kids at clinics about that. "How did you play so fast on such-and-such a tune?" I used to answer, "Well, fear was a primary motivating factor." I was 18 when I joined Kenton's band, and there were a lot of fast tempos. I just had to do it. Adrenaline took over, and in the process, I got behind a lot of technical 8-balls, because you just do whatever you have to do to make it work. I finally got hip to the idea that playing relaxed makes playing fast tempos much easier.

One thing I'm happy about is that I really like playing rolls now. I stayed away from them for years, because I thought that my roll was the worst. But when I was in Copenhagen with Weather Update, I took a snare drum lesson from Bent Lylloff, from the Royal Academy of Music. He's a great teacher, and he's very encouraging. By combining what he showed me with something Vic Firth told me a while back, I finally feel comfortable playing rolls again.

Joe Zawinul was cute. We played in Copenhagen that evening, and during the set, right in the middle of a tune, Joe announced, "Peter Erskine took a drum lesson today, and now he's going to show you what he learned," so I played a roll.

Practicing is certainly worthwhile if you can apply

what you've practiced. For example, the first time I went in to do a recording with a click, I was like, "Wow, what's this?" It really took some getting used to. But look at Dave Weckl. In addition to whatever intrinsic talents he has which are considerable- he also developed that whole Gary Chester approach, and geared himself towards playing with a click. So from the get-go, his recordings have been really impressive.

RM: I seem to remember a nice roll on the *Bass Desires* album.

PE: Yeah, on "Black Is The Color Of My True Love's Hair." But as far as rolls go, remember the PAS convention a couple of years ago when I played a piece for two drum sets and orchestra with Louie Bellson? Louie was remarkably generous, because if he wanted to apply the heat, he could play pretty serious circles around anybody. But there was a meeting ground as far as the musical level. He wasn't trying to turn it into a chops buster, which made it very comfortable for me. But the world is going to end with a whimper, not a bang, right? Louie got me with a whimper. At the rehearsal he told me, "At this point I'll play a roll, and you join me." Well, at the concert he played the softest roll I'd ever heard in my life. I glanced out in the audience and saw Jim Coffin from Yamaha, and he was already laughing. I turned to Louie and just shook my head no.

RM: A few minutes ago, when I asked you to analyze yourself, you said that you think you have a good backbeat. I would say that backbeat was what characterized a lot of the Weather Report *This Is This* album, especially the title tune and "The Man With The Copper Fingers." Those were pretty much rock 'n' roll songs.

PE: Kind of. A lot of Joe Zawinul's music is boogie-woogie, really. That's the kind of beat that he likes.

RM: I liked the simple little rock fills that you played in those two tunes. At the end of Santana's guitar solo on "Copper Fingers," you play straight triplets on the snare drum. It was simple, but it was great.

PE: Maybe it was great *because it was simple.* I was doing a rehearsal the other day, and the bass player said, "That's great, Pete. What are you playing?" I played the beat for him, and he said, "That's all it was?" I said, "Yes, I dare to be stupid." But with everything else that was going on, that beat fit perfectly.

RM: Buddy Rich was once quoted as saying that the best four-bar break anyone had ever played was something that Shadow Wilson did on a Basie tune called "Queer Street." When I got the chance to interview Buddy a couple of years ago, I asked him what was so great about that fill. His answer was that the fill itself was no big deal, but it was great because it was the perfect thing to play at that time. I guess that's why I liked your triplets so much. They were the perfect thing to play at that point in the song.

PE: A few years back, I was scared to death to play anything like that in Weather Report. Joe once said, "If I ever hear you play [sings 16th-note figure] around the toms, I'll kill you." So I was trying to think of all these ways to play something else. Most of the time, it was something way too busy.

I think I took his comment way too literally. If you feel that something is the right thing to play, you should play it. If someone tells you specifically, "We don't want that," that's one thing. But for most of us who are working for bandleaders or artists, making a musical contribution is what we're there for. So if you feel that what you're doing is musically valid, you've got to trust that. If you believe in something, you can make it irresistible. And a lot of times, even if a producer or somebody says, "Im not sure that this is good," and you say, "Yes, this is good," then people will say, "Okay."

RM: On the slow ballad "I'll Never Forget You," you start out playing short, staccato sounds with tight hi-hat and dry bass drum. As the tune continues, the sounds get fatter. Was that a conscious decision to do that, or do those things just come from instinct?

room for a whole lot of preconceptions.

I was recently talking to someone who asked me, "Did you think a lot about your playing before you did your solo album?" I had to be frank and say, "I didn't give it a thought. I was just worried about getting the tunes prepared, getting the studio we wanted, and hoping everyone would show up. I took it for granted that the playing would be okay." In fact, I

Billy Childs, Scott Colley, Peter and Joel Frahm at Monterey Jazz Festival rehearsing

Peter Erskine Library

PE: I remember that interview with Steve Gadd where he said that playing on top of or behind the beat is never a conscious decision. You just try to make the music feel good. That's pretty much the motivating factor for anything I play. I just try to respond to whatever the other musicians are playing. There's no

think we did get some real good performances, and that's a credit to the comradery and professionalism of the musicians. There's no substitute for experience. It was a good combination of players: guys like John Abercrombie, Marc Johnson, Bob Mintzer, Joe Lovano. Also, Vince Mendoza, who helped write a lot of the music and acted as co-producer, was a tremendous help. The other thing that I'm proud of is that we did it in two days. It's a lot of music-65 minutes-and we did it almost all direct to 2-track. The key thing in a situation like that is to know what you're going after and when it's time to move on. There's always the temptation to do one more take. But you can't be self-indulgent. You've got to get it-boom and move on. So the album has a very live feeling. I'm really happy with the drum sound on the album, which is coming out on Denon. It will initially be released on Compact Disc. At some point, Passport will release it on vinyl and cassette.

RM: Give me some background on the tune "Lions and Tigers and Bears."

PE: Vince Mendoza had sequenced this thing in step time, and he gave me a cassette of it, saying, "This might be good to play along with." So I spent one day listening to the thing through a Walkman and learned it. It's kind of a complicated sequence. Then I got the idea to do a drum solo in front. I didn't have a footswitch to start the sequence from the Macintosh, so Vince had to stand in the room with me, and he started it when I gave him a cue. I had to have the tempo locked in mentally so that, when we kicked in the sequence, it would match what I was playing. It turned out good. That was the second take.

RM: To me, it's interesting to hear this drum solo with a very human feel, and then suddenly this very mechanical sequence comes in over the top of it.

PE: It kind of grabs you and punches you in the nose. In the space of two days, I talked to two people about it. Vince said that the sequence wasn't loud enough; my dad said the drums weren't loud enough.

RM: By the time this appears in print, you'll be living in L.A. Do you have any immediate plans?

PE: I'm going to be writing music for *A Midsummer Night's Dream*. That music will have a very different tone from the music I did for Richard III. I'm really interested in theater, where the music is just one element that is combined with the language, the lighting, the set design-everything. For some time now, I've been interested in the study of film scoring, and I'm excited about the possibility of playing on some film scores in L.A. And I'm definitely going to follow this solo album up with another one, which will pursue the same thing: the combination of electronic and acoustic instruments. Playing electronic drums with an acoustic bass has a different quality, and I thought the

combination worked well.

RM: You didn't have the Yamaha electronic drums when you did the first Abercrombie album, but will you start using them with him now? I ask that because he's very involved with guitar synthesizer, so I wondered if the electronic drums might blend well with that.

PE: Maybe. I'm locked into a mind-set with John. I've always used the small jazz kit with the 18" bass drum with him, and I like that tonality with John's electronic stuff. I want to use the electronic stuff more, but I don't know what kind of music I'm going to be playing. I'm going to have to create just out of the necessity of whatever music I'm hearing in my head. I think it's time for that to blossom into something, and the electronics will be part of it. The musicians as yet are unknown.

Before I did my album, I didn't have a firm idea of what I expected my music to sound like. I do now. I have firm ideas about how I like the beat to lay, how I like the sound to resonate, and how I want my drums to sound. I can walk into a booth and say, "I don't like that sound. I want it more like this." It's not going to be the same every time, but I know what it can be and how I like it to be. I know what I want music to do.

RM: What's the difference between the Peter Erskine who moved to New York a few years ago and the Peter Erskine who is now moving back to L.A.?

PE: My first instinct is to say that I've come full circle. I was just thinking this morning about a demo record I made with Eliane Elias, Michael Brecker, and Eddie Gomez when I first moved to New York. It was great. The music really danced. I think I've come back to that. Being in New York and in Steps was transitional for me. I got the jazz thing more together and learned how to record better in a studio. I also got my dynamic spread more controlled, and I got more control of my limbs so that I didn't play with a jerky motion. Everything is smoother and more relaxed. I think I'll leave with kind of the same attitude that I came here with: I feel pretty fresh musically, and I'm looking forward to the music that I'm going to be playing.

Peter Erskine
1993 A Work In Progress

By Rick Mattingly

"There's a terrific chapter in this book about the sense of hearing," Peter Erskine says, reaching for A *Natural History Of The Senses* by Diane Ackerman. He's sitting in a multicolored stuffed chair ("A real Hollywood chair," he says, delighted by its sheer gaudiness) next to a grand piano. Out in the yard, his kids are constructing a fort from cardboard boxes that the new Yamaha drumset Peter had just secured for the upcoming Steely Dan tour arrived in.

"Here it is," he says, and then reads aloud: "'Polyphony coincided with the building of the great Gothic cathedrals, and the birth of harmony with the culmination of the Renaissance and the beginning of modern science and mathematics that is, the two great changes in our understanding of space.' "Then there is an asterisk," Peter says, "and an observation made by Pauline Oliveros. This is what caught my eye when I was reading this: 'Any space is as much a part of the instrument as the instrument itself.'

"What interested me," he says, laying the book aside, "was this whole thing about science and music. Coincidentally, I was reading another book called *Music Of The Spheres*, and it was tracing the development of music and science through the ages. During the time of Pythagoras, music and science were seen as two great ideals of how perfect the universe was-these natural laws and orders. Once you got into the Romantic age, with composers like Beethoven, music had become a much more subjective, personal expression, and science had started to understand that the world isn't such a perfect kind of place. Now science is studying chaos, and it certainly is a chaotic society." Erskine pauses a moment to let what he's said sink in. "I like the fact that you can express yourself so many different ways with music," he says.

"Going back to that thing about space being as much a part of the instrument as the instrument itself," he continues, "that was very true when we made the ECM recording *You Never Know*. In the room at Rainbow Studio in Oslo, we had a grand piano with the lid open, the drums were in the same room, there was no blanketing, no gobos [baffles.] I played the drums differently than I might have had I been in a drum booth with a lot of padding and isolation. Sonically, there were some physical restraints suggested by the space where we were making the music. On one hand it was inhibiting, and I knew I couldn't play the drums just any old way. But on the other hand, imposing a discipline in the artistic process can be very revealing and liberating."

Peter Erskine's speech often takes the form of a good musical composition. He'll start with an introductory theme (for instance, a quote from a book,) introduce the main theme (the second quote,) develop the material ("What interested me ...") resolve the development ("I like the fact...") and then resolve the primary theme (explain how the quote relates to his specific circumstances.) Similarly, just as Erskine's voice will drop to near whisper level when he is speaking of things he feels very strongly about, so too will the music he cares for the most be played at the softer end of the dynamic range, with a minimum of explosive cymbal crashes and accents.

It is sometimes said that life is not a destination, it is a journey, and those who get the most out of it are the ones who take the time to enjoy the trip and explore the side roads and scenery. The ultimate goal has more to do with discovering an interesting route and maybe blazing a few new trails along the way than in actually reaching a specific location. Consciously or not, Erskine lives that philosophy in the pursuit of his art. During the first few years of his career, he seemed to delight in making left turns. His first major gigs, with Stan Kenton at the age of seventeen and then with Maynard

Ferguson, suggested that he was going to follow a fairly mainstream jazz direction, albeit with a modern rock-influenced consciousness.

Fans and critics alike were astounded when he joined Weather Report, the reigning electric fusion band of the '70s, which featured keyboardist Joe Zawinul, saxophonist Wayne Shorter, and bassist Jaco Pastorius. But despite his longevity with the group, Erskine never quite became known as a fusion drummer, as he continually turned up in acoustic jazz combo settings on albums and in clubs. He even appeared on folk singer Joni Mitchell's tribute album to jazz bassist Charles Mingus, an album that totally defied categorization. Moving to New York in the early '80s, Erskine seemed to be moving in a hard-bop direction, notably with his early work in Steps Ahead, which featured saxophonist Michael Brecker, vibist Mike Mainieri, pianist Don Grolnick, and bassist Eddie Gomez, and on countless club gigs and record dates. But he also became fascinated with electronics and MIDI technology, and enjoyed doing jingle and soundtrack sessions in recording studios. And as Steps Ahead got mired in personnel changes and conflicting priorities, Erskine began working more and more with various combinations of New York-based jazz musicians such as guitarists John Scofield, Mike Stern, John Abercrombie, and Bill Frisell, saxophonists Bob Berg, Joe Lovano, and Bob Mintzer, trumpet player Randy Brecker, keyboardists Eliane Elias and Warren Bernhardt, and bassists Will Lee and Marc Johnson.

Erskine physically relocated to California in 1987, but musically he became a citizen of the world, spending increasing amounts of time touring and recording in Europe and Japan, maintaining his New York associations, and still managing to develop a presence in the clubs and recording studios of his home state. "I travel so much now that I feel comfortable playing pretty much anywhere I go," he says. "I'm like a tourist, and I try to fit in wherever I am. The drumming identity, I think, remains a constant. I'm not worried about maintaining some geographical agenda, like, 'This is the way we play in New York.' Who cares? Labels are confining-ultimately they can become dangerous." Paradoxically, as Erskine has spread himself over an ever-widening range of situations and styles, his musical identity has become stronger and more focused. Whether it's the freedom of his playing in

the acoustic-trio setting of his solo album *You Never Know*, the tight, precise traditional approach to big-band drumming on Bob Mintzer's *Departure*, the pop sensibility evident on Gary Burton's new album, *We Can Try Love Again*, which features vocalist Rebecca Parris, or the near anarchy of his playing on the upcoming John Abercrombie album on ECM simply titled, *John Abercrombie, Marc Johnson, Peter Erskine*. Erskine's drumming is marked by a consistency of approach that is all the more remarkable for not being based around signature licks and patterns. It's more of a feel and an attitude, in which the only goal is to serve the music.

But Erskine is quick to point out that his playing is not simply reactive. "I used to think that creative music making implied that I react to everything around me," he says. "But if you're not careful, you're commenting on everything that is played, which is one step away from Mickey-Mousing everyone else's ideas without contributing your own statements. You must also make statements that other people will play off of, because ideas have to emanate from all the instruments. "The other thing is that a lot of musicians, especially drummers, sometimes confuse creativity with busyness. They think, 'I'm being busy, so I'm being creative.' As any other drummer does, I have my own vocabulary of rhythms or patterns that I'm likely to express myself with. But you don't want things just rolling off the end of your sticks because you've spent so much time practicing them. "There are ways you can practice that will better prepare you for playing interactively while still observing the necessary space. For instance, record yourself playing some basic timekeeping in any musical style. When you first listen back to it, the tendency is to listen from a drummer's standpoint and notice how well you executed this or that and how interesting it was, and so on. "But try listening back and imagining that you have to play bass or piano along with it. Is there room for a bass or keyboard? You might start becoming aware that something larger needs to be honored. You have to serve the music. That requires putting a little bit of ego aside and playing for the tune. This is something the great pop drummers have known all along. The more I listen to Jeff Porcaro's drumming, the more I understand a drummer like Paul Motian. To me, there's a very strong connection because they both serve the music in their drumming."

Much of Erskine's own ability to serve the music comes from the fact that he is dealing with an incredibly wide range of resources. His conversation is punctuated with references to literature, art, science, and classical music. But he's also well aware of pop culture and tends to be up on the latest jokes. Likewise, as he makes his way through a piece of music, Peter will combine elements from a wide palette of influences and colors, feeling free to go off on tangents and make asides, secure that he will never lose sight of the main focus. But his ability to draw on so many sources is dependent on his willingness to discipline himself in terms of specific elements, as illustrated by a recent exercise in restricting his setup.

"One day," Erskine recalls, "I was watching a video of the Miles Davis Quintet of the early '60s with Tony Williams, and he was only using two cymbals. It was amazing! As I was watching and listening, I started wondering why I had all these other cymbals around me. I remembered my teacher in college, George Gaber, telling me that every once-in-a-while I should go out with just a snare drum, bass drum, hi-hat, and cymbal, explaining that if you can do the gig that way, you can do it that much better with the whole enchilada sitting there. I had a European tour coming up with Kenny Wheeler, so I made the decision to only take two cymbals." Not surprisingly, Erskine found that imposing that kind of discipline opened up new possibilities. "It forced me to develop more of a relationship with each cymbal," he explains. "A cymbal can function more than just one way: You can ride on it, you can crash it, you can do anything you want. You discover different tonal qualities, and your touch really gets a workout because when a soloist changes, you don't have a bunch of different cymbals to choose from. "I knew that one of the cymbals I would take would be a 22" Pre-Aged K because of the creamy kind of sound quality. But the second cymbal needed to have certain kinds of crash qualities as well as ride capabilities, so I called Lennie DiMuzio at Zildjian and explained the idea, and he sent me an 18" K ride that sounded cool when I crashed on it and also worked great as a ride cymbal. I put three rivets in it close together, which is an idea I got from Louie Bellson."

It wasn't just a matter of finding the right cymbals, though. Erskine's signature stick, made by Vic Firth, features a small, round tip, which he originally favored because it produced a consistent sound no matter at what angle the stick struck the cymbal, a valid consideration in a setup that contained a number of cymbals mounted at different heights. "At the time we designed that stick," Erskine recalls, "I was trying to get greater clarity in my playing, and that consistency of sound in the stick was helping me achieve a more pinpoint type of accuracy in my drumming. But now I was in a situation where I needed to broaden the textural possibilities of each cymbal, and I found that if I used a more traditional teardrop shaped bead, such as the Firth 7A, the sound could change as I angled the stick, depending on how much wood was coming in contact with the cymbal. You can get a more pinpointed sound by using the tip of the bead, or it can broaden out when you use the fatter section. "This presented a bit of a crisis," Peter admits, "because a lot of times I wasn't using my signature stick model. So I called Vic and told him that I was using a different stick, and he said, 'You're maturing as a player. Your stick was delivering a very specific sound, but now you're searching for a different quality.' "We don't want to cause too much confusion," Erskine says, "but we're working on a second design with a different tip. We don't want to abandon the original design because it's still valid, and I still use it for different situations. In fact, I've also been using the Buddy Rich signature stick for certain things. The fact that people use my stick really has nothing to do with my name being on it. You might originally be attracted to a signature stick because you're a fan of a certain player and it's part of the way he gets his sound. But ultimately the name is just an identifying factor, and people will only use it if it works for them."

Having met -and thoroughly enjoyed the challenge of using only two cymbals, Erskine has returned to a slightly larger setup. "I've added a third cymbal," he says. "It's usually a 16" or 18" K dark thin crash over on my right that I sometimes use as a ride. For recording, I'll break that rule (not that it's really a rule) and use various cymbals for different purposes. "I quoted Mel Lewis in my drum book a few years back, saying, 'Every cymbal I have is a ride. Every cymbal I have is also a crash.'" "I

First promo photo with Weather Report

Peter Erskine Library

know that my drumming has become more specific in terms of placement and ideas," Erskine responds. "I guess that's pretty accurate; the drumming functions more in terms of propelling the music along as opposed to crashing and accenting so much."

It's especially obvious on the aforementioned *You Never Know*, in which Erskine's playing is decidedly non-busy. He colors and shapes the music with a minimum of drum activity, relying primarily on a dancing ride cymbal to lead the music forward. "As simple as my playing is getting on one hand," Peter says, "on the other hand I'm really enjoying getting into finer subdivisions, little five and seven note groupings, and all sorts of two-three combinations within a 4/4 meter. By playing more simply, I feel like I'm opening myself up to much more stuff that I can play. In other words, the ECM album was an extreme of playing very openly and not playing a whole lot. But it opened my ears to all sorts of things I can play, and now I know how I can play actively on the kit while staying very relaxed and centered and keeping the clarity. But when I was just recycling this very limited number of drum devices that I had which is what I hear a lot of drummers do- it just clouded up the music. You have to go to the extreme and go through a period without playing very much.

"My father called me up and said, 'You owe it to your fans to play a little more on your next record,'" Peter says, laughing. "And the next album will have more in the way of drum activity. But this was an album of trio music, and I'm real pleased with the balance between the amount of commenting and the amount of space. More than anything else, I think there's a great clarity to the recording. I'm delighted with the way it came out. "One thing I wanted to do was make an album that didn't cause the listener to get up halfway through and turn it down because the volume suddenly jumped out of the speakers at you. In general, the volume level and texture of music has become so loud that it becomes a sort of wash. Anywhere you go in public there seems to be a musical soundtrack going, whether you ask for it or not. And with a lot of recordings or live groups, the starting point tends to be so loud that after a while your ears become numb to a lot of the ideas that are being expressed by the musicians."

Sadly, Erskine's appreciation for the softer end of the dynamic spectrum has been influenced, in part, by ear damage. "Goodness knows my ears have borne the brunt of a lot of musical excess over the years," Erskine admits. "Finally, a couple of years ago, I was doing a tour with Gary Burton and Pat Metheny. We were in New York for a week, doing two and sometimes three shows a night. I had also booked a lot of recording projects, and was in the studio recording eight to ten hours a day. Later, I was asking myself what I was trying to prove, and to whom? "Anyway, my ears weren't getting any kind of rest, and at the end of the week in the recording studio I suddenly heard this loud, oscillating frequency. I thought it was coming through the headphones, so I ripped them off, but the sound didn't stop. "I panicked," Peter says with controlled emotion, his voice betraying the fear he still feels when recalling the incident. "It finally stopped. Apparently, a muscle attached to the eardrum went into a spasm. The body will do what it can to protect itself, and I had pushed everything over the edge.

"I came back from the tour, and a few days later I noticed that the ringing in my ears hadn't gone away. In the past, my ears would ring after a gig, and I'd think, 'Wow, we were really loud tonight,' and the next day it would be gone. But that's ear damage at work. I already knew that I was losing certain frequencies in my hearing, because I was going to an ear doctor. Back when I was in Maynard's band, they molded hearing-protection plugs for me, but I didn't like wearing them because I felt it was throwing my dynamics off. Playing that loud, I should have been wearing them all the time, but I wasn't. "Anyway, the day I noticed that my ears were still ringing, a copy of Modern Drummer came in the mail, and it was the one with Rod Morgenstein's cover story where he dealt very candidly about how his ears had been damaged. I was very grateful that he talked about that, because when something like that happens to you, you are frightened, and it helps to hear someone else talking about it. "So I went to a couple of different ear doctors, and they confirmed that I had tinnitus. It's a very distressing thing, because I'm a guy who likes quiet, and my life has been robbed of one of its pleasures. The sound never stops. The shame is that, in some respects, I'm more enthused about music now than I've ever been, and yet another part of me is saying, 'When can I take a break?' because I've noticed that if I give my ears a rest periodically, the symptoms are sometimes less severe. "Now I try to practice whatever preventive maintenance I can. Seriously, you have to protect your hearing. If you don't want to go as far as molded plugs, which is what I use, then at least use those foam plugs that you can buy at any pharmacy. They can build amps that go to 11, but your ears can only go so far. I think we all have to be on a mission. I don't care if I sound like an old fart at this point, a lot of stuff is just too damn loud. Music is not meant to be listened to when it's that loud. You can't appreciate it.

Joseph Futterer/Richie Powell

'I love all the technological advances of the age of information, but I think a heavy price is being paid.

Before there was electricity, things quieted down when it got dark and people went to sleep. But now, everything is 24-hour, non-stop, in your face. MTV has created this quick-cut kind of mentality and expectation, and we have a very loud, noisy, offensive environment. People are being led to believe that they need constant input, but they don't. Constant input is wrong; there's no time for reflection. It just deadens people. And it messes up your hearing." Erskine has come to realize that audiences respond positively to music that is played at a reasonable volume. "When I went on tour with my trio, I insisted that we do a couple of tunes very soft," he says. "You have to get the cooperation of the sound people, because otherwise, when you start playing soft, they'll turn everything up. 'Hey, you still don't get it. Soft. I don't want it loud. I want people to hear the instruments from the stage.' You have to get them to go along with you on faith that it's going to work. "I could sense people leaning forward to listen, and then getting with it. We all realized that the audience was both hungry and grateful for that kind of dynamic shift, playing so quietly that it demands everyone's attention. And then when you increase the natural volume, it can be more effective. Palle Danielsson [bassist on *You Never Know*} told me he went to hear Ravi Shankar a few years ago, and when he got there, he was dismayed because there was little or no PA system. He said at first you had to strain to hear them, but you got acclimated to the volume level, and by the time the group reached their own fortissimo, it was hair-raising.

"On a similar note, I saw Jim Hall playing at a local jazz club here. He was doing this quiet guitar intro, but there were some loud talkers at a couple of the tables. Instead of turning up, though, he smiled this little rueful smile and I saw him turn down. People were still talking, so he turned down some more. Now he was playing really soft, and these people suddenly realized that they better shut up. He forced everyone to listen by getting softer, and it was brilliant.

"I'm going out with Steely Dan soon," Peter says, "and we'll be playing in some pretty large venues, so I imagine the volume will be more than what I've done lately. I'm going to wear molded ear monitors to prevent any further damage to my hearing. The system comes with an Aphex limiter to prevent any sound accidents, and it also means that I won't have monitor cabinets around me interfering with the drum sound." Erskine will be using a slightly larger drumkit for the Steely Dan tour, in terms of both number and sizes of drums. He's also taking two ride cymbals and four crashes. "I was talking to Colin Schofield at Zildjian," Peter says, "and he pointed out to me that in big rooms like the ones Steely Dan will be playing, subtle differences between two cymbals won't reach out too far. If you want a difference to be perceived out front, you have to be playing with bigger differences on stage. Crash cymbals have to be bigger and there has to be a greater difference in size and tonal quality between cymbals. So I'll be using a standard 20" K ride as my primary ride, and an 18" K Custom with three rivets in it as my other ride. The first time I played that cymbal was on a jazz record date, and interestingly enough it sounded like a cymbal you might have heard Ed Thigpen play with Oscar Peterson. But I know it's going to work well in the Steely Dan situation because it has an airy but precise sound.

"Speaking of the sound of a cymbal, there are some interesting things in this book about the sound of music and why a Stradivarius violin sounds good," Peter says, picking up *A Natural History of The Senses* again. "Here it is: 'Many violinists and violin makers insist that violins grow into their beautiful, throaty sound. A violin played exquisitely for a long time eventually contains the exquisite sounds within itself. Somehow the wood keeps track of the robust lyrical flights. In down-to-earth terms, certain vibrations made over and over for years, along with all the normal processes of aging, could make microscopic changes in the wood. We perceive those cellular changes as enriched tone. In poetic terms, the wood remembers.' "I feel that way about my instruments," Peter says. "Like the way you play a cymbal and break it in. I think molecules do get used to working a certain way. I could be full of baloney on this, but I don't like my cymbals to be played by other people.

"I was talking to Joe Montineri about this. He's pretty opinionated when it comes to drums, but he said he really liked my Yamaha maple drums. He said that in five years, when the maple really ages and settles, the drums are going to be that much greater. "I have an amazing drum that he made. It's a 4x10 ultra soprano snare drum. I sometimes set it up between my small tom-tom and my hi-hat. A lot of drummers like having a second snare drum for rifle-shot effects, but this drum has a delicate articulation that's great for rolls, and I won't hit it hard. I use it for tonal variety and rhythmic interplay."

Considering Erskine's former enthusiasm for electronic drums, it seems strange that he won't be using them in the Steely Dan setting, given the limitations of miking in large venues. Just what is Peter's relationship with electronic drums these days? "We're distant friends," he laughs. "I never call, I don't write... I don't send faxes ... "When I do composing projects I'll still trigger sounds from a Yamaha RY-30 using a drumKAT or a master keyboard, and I still like ddrums a lot. But as far as the Steely Dan tour, I realize that I could really beef up the drum sound if I were triggering, but that's not the idea. I want a simple setup that sounds great, so I'll just go with my Yamaha maple kit with the new *YESS* suspension system."

At the time of this interview, Erskine was preparing for the Steely Dan gig by practicing to the group's CDs. "It's neat playing along with a Bernard Purdie track, then with a Jeff Porcaro track, then a Rick Marotta track, and then a Gadd track, and noting the different placement of the backbeat," he says. "I'm really looking forward to the experience, because there are a lot of different responsibilities between playing a jazz gig and playing a show like this, where you do so many songs in an evening. I've done some pop-oriented things before, but this is big time. For all the different gigs I've done, I've never gotten the reaction from people like I get when I mention Steely Dan. It's one of those bands that people feel a connection with over the years. And for

Rehearsal for La La Land concert at Olympic Stadium in Seoul, Korea.

Peter Erskine Library

me, personally, in the late '70s the three hip things to listen to were Weather Report, Joni Mitchell, and Steely Dan, besides continually listening to Miles."

Despite the hearing protection, bigger drums, and louder volume required by bigger halls, Erskine has no plans to bash his way through the Steely Dan concerts. "I notice that when I start hitting the drums harder," he explains, "I feel less freedom than when I'm playing at a sonic-level I'm comfortable with. It has to do with textural clarity. Right after I got called to do the gig, I got nervous for a second because I was flipping channels one day and I saw this rock concert where it looked like everything was really loud, and I hoped Steely Dan wouldn't be like that. But as I prepare for the gigs, the reference point I use is Jim Keltner, because he doesn't hit the drums that hard, but it sounds big. I've been listening a lot to the Little Village recording, and it's so cool. The music dances beautifully. Jim is an amazing drummer. It's like Dixieland rock drumming," Peter laughs. "Keltner is the Zutty Singleton of rock. So evoking this sonic image of Jim Keltner is kind of an energizing and comforting reference point for me." Given the fact that Keltner began his career as a jazz drummer, it would seem logical that Erskine would hear something in Keltner's time feel that he could relate to so well. "By the same token," Peter says, "I think Jeff Porcaro inherited a lot of his father Joe's jazz sensibility and emotion, and that comes through on the Steely Dan records Jeff played on. That's the really hip thing about Steely Dan; there are a lot of jazzy elements in their music.

"There can be great creativity within basic, simple beats," Erskine insists. "Creativity doesn't just come from constant variations in a very obvious manner. The great pop drummers are not trying to reinvent the beat every few bars. But they are being very creative through small, incremental changes. Jeff Porcaro explained this brilliantly in the video he made. It's the subtle wave he had going on his hi-hat when he was playing a beat. There's a world of variation just in the way he opened and closed the hi-hat, even though the basic beat remained pretty much the same. It gave his playing a certain roll that made his drumming a compelling listening experience."

Erskine's description of Porcaro's playing could very well explain his own drumming on Gary Burton's new album, We Can Try Love Again. On "Our Love Is Here To Stay," Erskine maintains a steady, pop-like backbeat through the bulk of the tune. But listen closely to his hi-hat and you'll hear those subtle variations that give his playing an ebb and flow. "I was digging playing very simply and not varying things too much," he says about the album. "When I was younger, I felt the need to always leave a few fingerprints at the scene of the crime. But I can play a tune now and not feel that urge. Just the touch and the placement of the beat should reveal that it's me playing, and I don't otherwise feel that I have to call too much attention to it."

A similar attitude is evident on the Bob Mintzer Big Band album *Departure*, on which Peter plays four of the tracks. There are countless places where Erskine could have engaged in explosive punctuations and snazzy set-ups for horn figures, but by and large he doesn't, preferring instead to sound (at times) like he's playing the tune for the first time. "We'll run down sixteen bars to get the feel and then put it down on tape. I love that. Of course, you can always learn to play a piece of music better and better, but the first time you play something, there is a sense of freshness and discovery that is very revealing and honest. John Riley plays a lot with Bob's band in New York, and he sounds beautiful on the other tracks on the album. So I'm glad Bob lets me come in and play on a few tunes, because I still enjoy big band, especially when it's as good as Mintzer's band."

At the opposite end of the precision involved in the Mintzer Big Band is the looseness of the John Abercrombie Trio. Erskine, Abercrombie, and bassist Marc Johnson have played together so long that each is free to explore the music at will, trusting that it will all come out right in the end. On a soon-to-be-released recording by the trio along with saxophonist John

Surman, there are times when the musicians seem to be playing simultaneously more than playing together, and yet there is a sense that they are connected. "That's because we were not playing the music in box-like shapes," Peter explains. "We weren't worried about landing together on downbeats. It has a very free, kind of slippery feel, but it's not random. The velocities connect. It's like four rivers of mercury, occasionally joining together and then breaking apart. There is some very generous music making throughout that recording that's built on trust and a little bit of letting go." One track features a Johnson bass solo that Erskine accompanies with classical sounding figures that evoke images of percussion parts by Varese or Bartok. "If you think of making music in the kitchen," Erskine says, "Bartok is definitely there in the knife drawer, right next to Stravinsky and Varese. I love 'Ionization' [Varese] and 'Sonata For Two Pianos And Percussion' [Bartok] and any number of Stravinsky pieces. I think that listening to composers such as Beethoven, Haydn, Bach, and Mozart will give you a greater understanding of musicality and form, but drum-wise, there are going to be more obvious quotes from composers like Bartok and Varese than from Mozart."

Peter Erskine Library

For all of the influences inherent in Erskine's drumming, it is remarkably free of predictable licks or generic beats and timekeeping patterns. Sometimes, it almost seems as if he is making it up from scratch as he goes along, and yet there is a deep sense that Peter's drumming is built solidly on tradition. "My playing has changed in any number of ways over the past twenty years," he says. "Hopefully, what's happening whether it's big band or trio or free or not free is that I'm serving the music. I have as much ego as anybody, but I really do hold serving the music as the ideal. Because if I've approached something that way, I can listen to it for years afterwards and say, 'The music sounds good.'

"Back when I was first starting to make records with Weather Report, I would wonder if Steve Gadd ever heard them, but whenever I would run into him, he'd never say anything. Then one day he complimented me on my drumming on a Michel Colombier recording, on which I played very disciplined and relatively simple. It took a while for that to sink in, but it was very instructive because it wasn't the 'burning' kind of drum track that got his attention. He was already aware of the importance of playing to serve the music. "So whether you play fast or slow or busy or not, if it's serving the music at hand, then it's right. And there is no real mystery as to what the drums should do. Happily, more and more, I don't have to wonder what to play. The music will always give you a clue if you open up to it.

"Obviously, drummers have to practice basic techniques so they're not sitting there at a complete loss as to how to hit the drums or how to execute particular rhythms. But practicing just reinforces the 'I,' and after you've developed coordination on the instrument and learned your beats, you have to let the sound of the music guide you and allow that to determine what you're actually going to play. You have to learn not to use your normal drum devices and avoid that kind of macho posturing you see in certain types of music, where players are just rapid-firing as many notes as possible. That kind of music isn't really about listening."

"Playing is the more assertive part of the musical process, the masculine side of it, if you will. Listening is a more feminine trait, and would be regarded as the more passive musical experience. But we need to develop the female part of our musical psyche and learn to listen, because that's really the key to making music. When we truly learn to listen to what's going on around us, that's when we become better musicians."

Peter Erskine

2016 Playing With Intent

By Rick Mattingly

Peter Erskine's career has been like a highway that is constantly under construction, with numerous detours, side roads, bridges, sharp curves, hills and intersections.

Former *Modern Drummer* senior editor Rick Mattingly has probably spent more time in the legendary drummer's presence than any other journalist. To this day, their conversations are illuminating, surprising, and, above all, inspiring.

Peter Erskine's career has been like a highway that is constantly under construction, with numerous detours, side roads, bridges, sharp curves, hills, and intersections. That road has traversed a wide, scenic landscape, and while jazz has always been the primary itinerary, Erskine has traveled into other areas as well, reflected by his discography of more than 700 albums also encompassing pop, film scores, and classical projects. He's savored every twist and turn, and for those of us who've been following that journey for over forty years, it's been a fascinating ride. Consider some of the landmarks. After studying at the Interlochen Arts Academy, Erskine began his professional career at age eighteen, when he joined Stan Kenton's big band. After three years on the road with Kenton, Erskine reenrolled at Indiana University to continue his studies with the legendary percussion teacher George Gaber. A year later Peter left school to join Maynard Ferguson's band, which was a logical follow-up to the Kenton gig. But then he joined the electric fusion group Weather Report, which astounded those who had typecast him as "just" a big band drummer. During breaks with Weather Report, Erskine appeared on several small-group acoustic jazz albums, and then moved to New York to join Steps Ahead, which started out as an acoustic jazz combo but soon moved into the world of MIDI and electronics. On the side he did some studio work ranging from film soundtracks to commercial jingles to jazz dates, and he began releasing solo albums with various personnel and instrumentation. After moving to California, Erskine continued recording with a variety of artists and began leading his own trios, which recorded for the ECM label. Much of that music was the antithesis of his earlier loud, energetic drumming, featuring a very nuanced and spacious way of playing. But in between work with his own groups, he performed and/or recorded with such pop artists as Steely Dan, Boz Scaggs, Mary Chapin Carpenter, Elvis Costello, Kate Bush, and Joni Mitchell. He also began playing drum set in orchestral settings, notably in compositions by Mark-Anthony Turnage, including *Blood on the Floor* for jazz ensemble and orchestra; *Scorched*, dedicated to guitarist John Scofield; *Fractured Lines*, a double concerto for drumset and percussion (the latter handled by Evelyn Glennie); and *Erskine: Concertante for Drum Set and Orchestra*. Apart from playing, Erskine wrote several drumset method books for Hal Leonard and Alfred, made some instructional videos, authored a book titled *No Beethoven*, which uses Weather Report as a framework for his life, and started a record label, Fuzzy Music, on which he's released solo albums, projects by others, and innovative play-along apps. He's received two Grammy Awards, plus an honorary Doctor of Music degree from Berklee College of Music. And since 2000 he's been teaching at the University of Southern California

Thornton School of Music.

I first met Erskine in 1977, when he was with Ferguson, and over the years we've done several interviews and worked on some other projects together. I've always found it stimulating to spend time with Peter, because he's always excited about the new music he's doing, or the new way he's approaching music he's played before, or the new cymbal he's added to his setup, or the book he's just read that has offered a new perspective on music—even if the book had nothing to do with music per se. He has the depth that comes only from a wealth of experience and a lifetime of exploration, yet in terms of enthusiasm he's still the same guy I met in 1977.

MD: Some things seem to be coming full-circle in your life. You recently did a big band album with Patrick Williams called *Home Suite Home*, and you've released a big band app. On your new solo album, *Dr. Um*, you do a lot of groove playing, which you did plenty of in the past in a variety of settings. And a four-CD set, *Weather Report: The Legendary Live Tapes*, which documents much of the time you were in the band, was released recently.

Roberto Cifarelli/Peter Erskine Library

Peter: About three quarters of the Weather Report set came from my own cassette collection, which has been digitized. I used to give our soundman my portable cassette deck and ask him, "How about recording tonight's concert?" I wanted to document that stuff.

The thing I like about *Dr. Um* is, I've done the funk thing, I've done the fusion thing, but never as cool as the way I now seem to be playing. I've never had more fun playing than I'm having now. And it's odd, because, as I talk about in the *No Beethoven* book, we tend to think of ourselves as our young selves. We're always in the "now," and I don't realize until I catch a glimpse of myself in the mirror that I'm not in my twenties. So it's nice to feel creatively relevant and vital. I've been very busy, traveling and recording. It's as if I'm harvesting all the planting and growing I've done over the years. It's almost overwhelming.

LAST CHANCE! WIN A $3,695 PRIZE PACKAGE

MODERN DRUMMER

THE WORLD'S #1 DRUM MAGAZINE

UNCOMMON TIME
MAKE 4/4 SOUND LIKE MORE!

PETER ERSKINE
FROM WEATHER REPORT TO DR. UM
"THE SLEIGHT OF HAND IS MORE SUBTLE NOW"

40 YEARS

KENNY ARONOFF CATCHING UP

CARTER McLEAN BROADWAY'S *THE LION KING*

JON ANDERSON A DIFFERENT VIEW

JUNE 2016

Mutsy Erskine

MD: On many of your solo albums over the past few years, you were playing very sparsely; you weren't necessarily playing "time" in some tunes, yet there was always a sense of a time feel and forward motion.

Peter: That's playing with intention.

MD: How did the groove stuff that you'd played inform your ability to do that?

Peter: The job of the drummer is to provide rhythmic information to the band and the listener. How we do that is a matter of choice. Sometimes that choice is dictated by the stylistic demands of the music; other times it's an intuitive response to what you hear from the musicians you're working with. A musician who spends enough time playing time is then able to play with the time in such a way that forward motion can be clearly felt even if you're not playing, for example, a steady quarter-note pulse, because each note you play is informed by that experience. If you're just imitating free playing without understanding it contrapuntally—which is how I used to play free—then the foundation isn't there, and it doesn't take much of a breeze to come along and blow the house down, as it were.

So playing with intention became the thing that I needed to learn, and that became the guiding principle of what I called "anti-drumming." I was inspired by a film documentary called *Light & Shadow*, which is about directors of photography. At one point they interview the director of photography for the film *Rosemary's Baby*. He describes a scene where you're looking down a hallway into a bedroom, and Mia Farrow is sitting on the bed talking on the phone. The director, Roman Polanski, told him, "I only want to see the back of her head with the phone on her ear; don't show her face." During the premiere, that scene came on, and they saw everyone in the audience lean their heads to try to look around the corner to see her face.

To put that in more concrete musical terms, in James Brown's "Mother Popcorn," there's an open beat on 4, and you can't help but shake your booty to fill that vacuum. Nature abhors a vacuum, right? So the genius of James Brown, or of filmmakers or poets, is leaving things unsaid. What you don't play makes it an interactive listening experience for the other musicians and your audience.

That became kind of the cornerstone of my "anti-drumming" thing. It wasn't really "anti" drumming, but I was trying to figure out how to create those same kinds of moments by not being so implicit to where there is no role for the listener's imagination. If I do that with a firm grasp of the subdivisions, that stuff is all implied. everyone still talk about as being his most incredible break? It's the one on "Love for Sale," when he plays this startling single-stroke roll on the snare and stops. And then the band comes in. It's thrilling. You've just been taken to the edge of the abyss. You hear the audience react in delight. He took everyone's breath away for a second.

Meinl Percussion

If things get too explicit, the music loses a lot of charm. That's why I think space is a dynamic and interesting thing. But you have to respect it and not treat space like it's something to rush through as quickly as possible.

I don't know how concerned a lot of fast drumming is with space. And, of course, when you think of fast drumming you think of Buddy Rich. What does

So that's the kind of thing that fascinated me. But when you play the drums, people want to hear you play the drums. I explored the "anti-drumming" thing as far as I could figure out how to take it, and I was even beginning to regard myself as less of a drummer. I would listen to Tony Williams or Jack DeJohnette and find myself thinking, *THERE'S a drummer. I'm an*

accompanist. I wouldn't even dare put myself in the same category as "drummer" with those guys. But now I'm feeling more and more like a drummer.

MD: I remember a John Scofield CD in the '80s where you played a funk tune, and I was impressed with how flowing it was. The pulse was steady, but there was looseness in the subdivisions. With so many drummers then, every 16th was metronomically perfect, but it often sounded stiff.

Peter: When I was with Steely Dan, the bassist, Tom Barney, once said, "Hey, you're swinging the 16ths." I wanted to raise my hand and say, "Guilty as charged," but for Steely Dan's music, he was right. I tried to get it more stylistically correct, but swing is pretty hard for me to get away from. Swing is not so much a triplet feel—it's more of a legato thing. If we listen to a fast bebop line, like a Charlie Parker melody, it swings, right? But you'd be hard pressed to find a triplet in there. Now think of the Lawrence Welk theme song. That was explicit triplets—and that ain't jazz; that's Squaresville. So the phrasing becomes essential, because what we're really doing is accenting the offbeat, and more importantly the notes are connected in a legato sense. It's the legato phrasing that really makes something swing.

Now, the ride cymbal pattern is going to be closer to a triplet: ding, ding-a-ding, ding-a-ding. Here's where everything comes together in this beautiful full-circle moment. The rhythm is from Africa through the Afro-Caribbean portal, where the two and the three start to rub, and that rub is what swings. So the two/three interrelationship is the mystery, the thrill, the excitement, the beauty of this music. It's what makes anything feel great. That gets us into the areas of intention: how we are conceiving of the music, and then what's played and what isn't played.

I've been having my students play melodies just on the snare drum, either with brushes or sticks, and make it swing—oftentimes reducing it to one hand on the hi-hat. If you can swing a band with one hand on the hi-hat or with just brushes on the snare drum, you can swing. That takes me back years ago, seeing Jeff Hamilton. The music was swinging like crazy, and Jeff was just playing on a snare drum. We're the same age; we went to college together, but I remember thinking, *I want to be able to do that when I grow up*. I could see that this was a very mature way of playing.

MD: The first time I heard Jimmy Cobb live, I'd never heard anything swing so hard, and he was mostly playing quarter notes on the ride with just an occasional "swung" note.

Peter: We did "The Music of Miles" with Gil Evans a number of times at the Hollywood Bowl, and Jimmy Cobb played some of the *Porgy and Bess* stuff—quarter notes on the ride with that fat cross-stick on beat 4. It blows your mind because it swings so much. About three years later we're playing it at Disney Hall, but Jimmy Cobb isn't on that concert. One of the *Porgy and Bess* things is "It Ain't Necessarily So," and Terence Blanchard is dealing—he's playing. It would be very tempting to start tangling with that because it's so cool, but I only played quarter notes on the cymbal with a cross-stick on the snare. It was a long improvisation; Terence was soaring. We finish the tune, the place goes nuts, and what does Terence do? He walks back to me and pulls my hand up like I'm a champion boxer. I was just doing what Jimmy Cobb did, but it worked so great—that intuitive, magical brilliance of Jimmy Cobb.

I've worked a lot with Seth MacFarlane, who everybody knows from *Family Guy*. But he's a great singer and puts on a good show, and he always talks about the great arrangers and refers to the time when music was more than someone dicking around on a laptop. I did a record with Seth, *Music Is Better Than Words*, and we were recording direct to analog tape, so we either got a good take or we did it again. The first take was pretty much for running the tunes down, so I'm just playing quarter notes on the ride cymbal, hi-hat on 2 and 4, and I have a pencil in my left hand so I can mark certain brass figures on the part. We listen back, and I notice the chart is swinging like crazy. So we do the next take. I had all the rhythms marked, and I was doing my perfect Alvin Stoller imitation with a bit of Shelly Manne, with all the setups and little fills, and we finish the take and everyone's like, "That's it—a perfect take!" But then we were listening back, and I turned to the bass player, Chuck Berghofer, and I said, "This doesn't swing as much as that first run-through," and he said, "Yeah, you're right."

So I went up to Seth and the arranger/producer, Joel McNeely, and I said, "Hey, guys, can we do one more?" Seth was having fun singing with a big band, so he said, "Sure!" Joel said, "Okay, but why?" I said, "I think we can get it to swing more." The trumpet players were not happy about having to do it again, but we did it, and with the exception of a couple of spots here and there, I just played quarter notes on the ride and hi-hat on 2 and 4. No cross-stick, no setups, and it was that idea of not providing all the information, which invites the listener in and it becomes a participatory experience, as opposed to playing everything. That, to me, is not very interesting. This final result swung like crazy.

MD: There's a tune on *Dr. Um* called "Hawaii Bathing Suit" that features a sax-and-drums duet, and your playing in that section reminds me of Elvin Jones. Were you consciously thinking Elvin, or is that just part of your vocabulary that comes out in certain situations?

Peter: I was aware of it as I was playing. Tenor sax and drums—of course you're going to think of Elvin, and there is some specific Elvin vocabulary. But the beginning of the tune is the way I would play it, albeit you can hear the Tony Williams, Mel Lewis, and Jack DeJohnette influence as well. That's the fun thing: All those guys are in there. But without denying their influence, it sounds like me at this point. Elvin is going to be part of my drumming no matter what I do—the profound spirit of the man and the impact and influence his drumming had on me since I was eight or nine years old. He's like a drumming father, and while I can't claim that we had that close of a relationship, we were good friends, and I adore his drumming. I wish I understood it better, but that's part of why I like it so much. I'm only willing to study it so far, because I love having the mysterious relationship in terms of having to do it by ear. Nobody will ever play the way he did, but the magic of Elvin is still with us. Even though we can't

**From left top row: Jim Cox, Elvis Costello, Peter Erskine.
Bottom row: Will Lee, Burt Bacharach, and Vince Mendoza and orchestra at Capitol Studios.**

hug him and get soaking wet from one of his sweaty embraces…

MD: And come away drenched in the aroma of his aftershave…

Peter: [laughs] But he's as alive as at any time. He's always available, thanks to recordings. If there's a definition of heaven, I think it might be being in the minds, ears, hearts, and thoughts of others.

MD: On the Patrick Williams *Home Suite Home* album, "That's Rich" is dedicated to Buddy Rich. You told me that you asked if he could make it a tribute to Mel Lewis instead. Meanwhile, on the third movement of "Home Suite Home" there are a lot of open spots for drums, and your fills are very simple—more in the spirit of Mel than of, say, Buddy or Louie Bellson.

Peter: Playing like Buddy has always been "out of my wheelhouse," as they say. Every time I hear Buddy I love it, and it's thrilling, and I appreciate him more and more the older I get. But I was really struggling to figure out how to do "the Buddy thing." Pat told me to just play what I wanted, but I felt a responsibility to the intent of the piece, so I felt I had to try a little bit of the Buddy-isms. I was kind of smearing lipstick all over myself on that. But yeah, my general instincts are to play more simply. A couple of years ago Pat's band played a gig in L.A., and the woman who booked the band kept offering us glasses of wine. I had a bit too much wine and was playing a bit more gregariously than normal. I realized that I had overplayed. The next night I played the way I would normally play. After the first tune, I heard the lead trumpet player say, "Heeee's back!" The band noticed it. The night before, they had to deal with a drummer who was fighting them and the music. Normally I serve it up on a silver platter and try to make it as easy as possible.

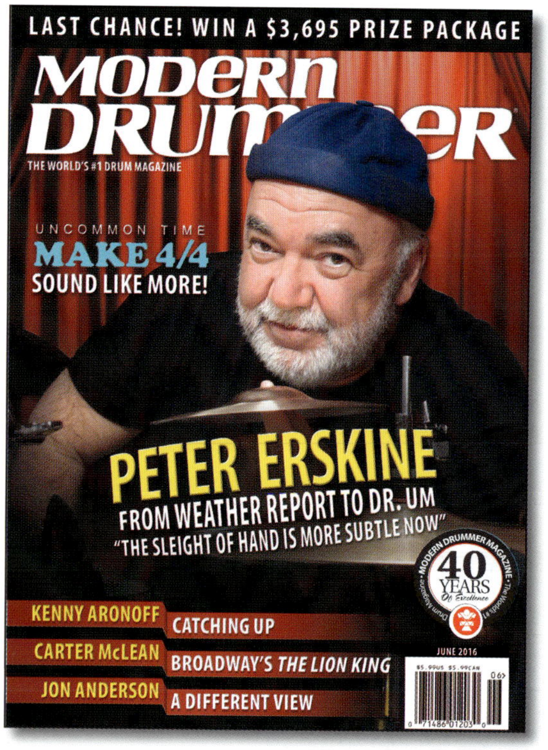

MD: There is an energy on some of the *Dr. Um* tunes that is comparable to a lot of the tracks on the new live Weather Report set. But with Weather Report, you were beating your brains out, and now you're playing with much less physical force but still achieving energy and momentum. Did you have to hit the drums that hard with Weather Report to generate that kind of energy, or was it just a matter of matching the volume of the keyboards and bass?

Peter: The stage volume was very loud. But I also played hard with Maynard's band, and when I look at video from that time period, I was hitting the drums

The Motivation Was Musical: Erskine on his Switch to Tama

Peter Erskine was as surprised as anyone when he switched to Tama drums. "For years, I paid no attention to Tama," he admits. "Tama drums seemed to be designed for a segment of the drumming population that I felt had no relevance to what I do."

But a couple of years ago, while attending a NAMM Show, Erskine walked by the Tama booth and saw Terry Bissette, at that time the sales manager for the company, whom he had known for years. "Terry asked if I would like to try out the new Star drums," Peter recalls, "so I sat down, but with all the noise I didn't get much of an impression. Then Terry contacted me a few months later and asked if I would like to try out the drums for real. He told me, 'We respect your relationship. We would just like your feedback on the drums.' I suggested that if they would pay my cartage guy for the use of his space and his time, we could do it at his warehouse and compare the Tama kit to several other drumsets. Hearing the Tama drums next to all the others, they sounded more musical."

That night, Erskine took the Tama kit to his gig at a jazz club, and he asked his wife to come by. "She came up to me at intermission and said, 'I really like the way these drums are making you play.' So I spent some more time with the Tama kit in various playing situations, and it seemed to bring out something in my playing that had been absent for a while.

"When I was with my previous company, I realized something was missing," Erskine explains. "I didn't know what it was, but I bought some vintage Gretsch, Rogers, and Slingerland drumsets, and it was like, 'Yeah, this is what I remember; this is what I like.' The Star kit is doing all that, and I don't seem to have to work as hard with it. Also, when I traveled, it was sometimes difficult to get one of the kits I was endorsing wherever I went, and I was running into some pretty nice drumsets here and there. So I was unfaithful in that relationship. And pretty emphatically—and stiffly too. I didn't realize at the time how much it was preventing me from playing what I was hoping to play. Things were coming out choppier than I was imagining. I went into the Weather Report gig as I've gone into a lot of things, with a wide range of combined influences, and I think I was still trying to sort some of them out.

If we compare the recording of "Speechless" on *Dr. Um* with the one on the album titled *Weather Report*, which was the last one [bassist] Jaco Pastorius and I made with the band, the drum part on *Dr. Um* is a little better measured, and there's only one moment where the drums kind of break out of this stoic quarter-note character. It just seemed the time to play something like that, and it was kind of a magical moment in the *Dr. Um* version. Because of the time stretching that happens, you almost catch your breath, and then all is well again. But I play those kinds of things differently now from the way I did when I was younger. Back then it was more a flurry of punches, and now the sleight of hand is more subtle.

Lissa Wales/Peter Erskine Library

MD: You've been teaching at USC for a while. What do today's students know that we didn't know, and vice

if you're unfaithful, relationships are going to change."

Still, Erskine didn't take the idea of a new endorsement lightly. "Any switch from one product to another has to be based primarily on sound, playability, and feeling a rapport with that ecosystem a drum brand has in terms of how the hardware works with the drum sound," he explains. "Along with that is the interpersonal factor and how you get along with everyone at the company. Without going into too much detail, it seemed like everything came together, and combining that with the fact that I was sixty years old, which is a bit of a turning point, my wife and I agreed that I should play what I want to play from here on out. I'd even toyed with the idea of withdrawing from all product relationships and just mixing and matching different brands of cymbals and drums. But I believe I've found home in terms of drums. I'm taking chances; I'm playing things I haven't played in a long, long time, along with things I've never played."

How, specifically, are different drums affecting what Erskine plays? "Drumming is all about making choices," Peter replies. "So an instrument that is immediately responsive and joyful to play prompts you to play more…er…joyfully. You experiment, your touch changes a bit, you're exploring. At first it might be the newness, but I've been playing Tama drums for over a year now, and every time I play these drums it feels like Christmas morning.

"There's always a lot of cynicism when you change an endorsement, and I get it. People think there is some sort of compensation when you move to a different company. My only compensation is that I'm getting to play a really remarkable instrument."

Erskine is also excited about some new Zildjian cymbals. "Paul Francis has come up with this new line that replicates A Zildjian cymbals from the 1950s," he says. "It's a mind-blower. It's like being given the gift of youth and time travel."

versa?
Peter: In general, the level of playing ability I see is astonishingly good across all genres and styles. I see drummers doing things that none of us dreamt of doing when we were young, whether it's gospel or speed metal or whatever. So the boundaries have been pushed, and the equipment is better and helps players do things. For instance, we didn't have double pedals back then.

The on-demand access that students have to finding just about any recorded performance—audio or video—is beyond *Star Trek*. When we were young, we had to be lucky enough to be in front of the TV when someone would broadcast jazz. But there were a lot more jazz clubs back in the day. I got to see Art Blakey when I was a kid, as well as just about every drum hero I was hoping to see. Those opportunities are harder for young people to come by.

They also establish a different kind of relationship with the music they listen to than we did. For example, when you and I were growing up and we bought an LP, we bonded with that record. We read the liner notes, we studied the photos, we got to know every note of that album. We had a deeply personal relationship with that recording. That's not possible when you have an iPod or an iPhone with 10,000 tunes in it. You've got so much availability, but some of the intimacy is gone.
MD: So instead of having relationships with albums, kids today are just "hooking up" with songs?
Peter: [laughs] Exactly! I sense that a lot of students haven't bonded with any particular style. We're really in mish-mosh land right now. So I'm trying to direct their listening. It's very subjective, but I try to get them turned on to finding specific things and digging deeper and deeper. And the beauty of today is that they can find stuff that we would have had a hard time getting our hands on.

MD: Nancy Zeltsman told me about students who come to Berklee to major in marimba, and they've never heard a live marimba concert. They've only seen people play on YouTube.

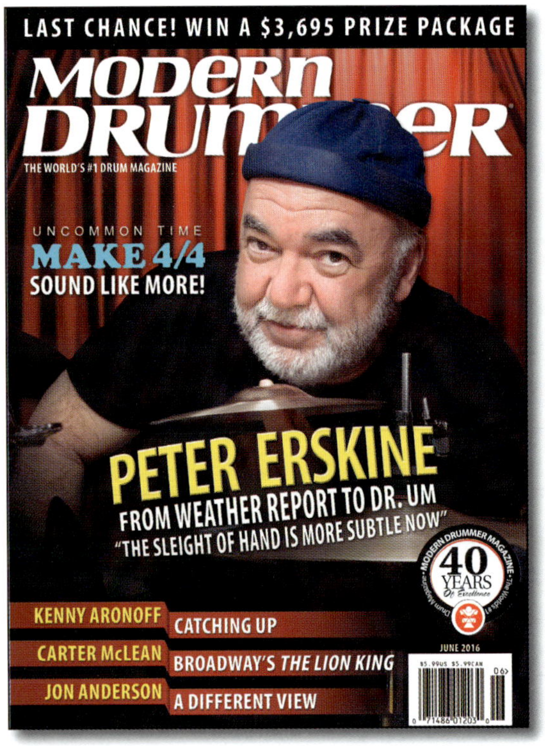

Peter: Today's students don't know what it was like to sit in front of Art Blakey's drumset and hear him do a press roll into a bass-drum/crash-cymbal downbeat. There was something about hearing Blakey do that in person that was life changing. The same with hearing Elvin or Mel Lewis play in person. Today's students don't get to hear as much music live as we did—that turn-on of seeing people who did this for a living. Even if you didn't like something, it helped you form a sense of discrimination: "That's not as hip as this other thing." I think young students today are as talented or more talented than we were. But we were lucky that we got to hear so much stuff live. Other than that, we didn't enjoy any "secrets"; we got to hear the stuff played live and then we tried to get that same effect when we played. And you can't get that through a computer screen or an iPod.

MD: You've done a lot of work with symphony orchestras over the past twenty years. When you went back to Indiana University and studied with George Gaber, did you feel that learning classical percussion would ever become relevant to your career as a jazz drummer?
Peter: I imagined that I might get to use that knowledge in the studio, and in New York that's what broke me into the jingle scene, because I could play orchestra bells. But when I went to IU, I felt that the primary benefit would have to do with touch. Oftentimes in my lessons, George Gaber would hand me a triangle beater or a bass drum mallet, point to the instrument, and say, "Mezzo-piano. You've got one chance. Play the best note you can—the most accurate dynamically, with the best tone." That was fascinating to me, the idea of being able to know your touch and your instrument so you could get the right sound immediately and it wasn't left to chance.

For too many years my playing was defined, as far as I was concerned, by a lot of good musical ideas and good intentions that never really saw the light of day because of things that got in the way, like my lack of touch, my lack of understanding the instrument, or my lack of technique. Now I'm feeling a lot closer to the intention being realized. One would hope that by the time you're sixty you have gotten a little bit closer to that.

I talk about this in *No Beethoven*: Can we still keep getting better as we get older? I can't help but look at the careers of many of my drumming heroes and compare which ones managed to stay relevant and grow, which ones stayed on a certain strata, and which ones just signed drumheads after a while. Then you see Steve Gadd, who's like a young kid again. I'm hearing new stuff coming out of Steve that's thrilling. He's playing with that same spark that I associated with him years ago when I first saw him play. I saw Wayne Shorter recently, and it blew my mind how masterfully he commanded the musical moments with his quartet. He's still evolving. So it is possible to keep getting better, and there is a responsibility, I think, because we get a lot out of this—a lot of joy, we get to make a living—but art is definitely a two-way street and a commitment, and we have to stay healthy and vital and involved and interested and caring and compassionate and open and all the things that artists are supposed to be: idiotic, selfish, crazy, sane, giving. You can't just sit back. It's too boring, and nobody cares.

Peter Erskine Library

EQUIPMENT

Peter Erskine: Gear Talk

By Mark Griffith

After a long session for the soundtrack of *Sing Pt. 2*, Peter was excited to talk about the evolution of his equipment and gear choices. But first, he wanted to address the myths of endorsements.

There is giant misconception out there about drum endorsements that I would like to clear up. People can be cynical if they choose, God knows there are enough things around that you can be cynical about. But the idea that any drummer plays any brand of drum set because they are receiving cash payments is a thought that I would like to dispel immediately. It's just not true. The unfortunate irony is that in many instances, it is after a drummer has struggled to reach a certain level of success and popularity, that he or she is approached about endorsements and when musical equipment is supplied at no charge.

In the case of Zildjian, the cymbals that the company sends me still belong to Zildjian. In the past I have requested the company's blessing to sell off some of the old cymbals that I have amassed in our 50 year relationship. In those cases, 100 percent of the proceeds from those sales have gone directly to a charity or a good cause, but none of those cymbals "technically" belonged to me.

In the case of Yamaha, they would send me drum equipment, and at the end of every tax year I would get a 1099 form and I had to declare the net worth of that equipment as taxable income. So in the end, if you compared it to going into Manny's and buying stuff at 40% off list price, it was very comparable. But the convenience of having equipment delivered to you anywhere in the world, and the support that Yamaha gave you with supplying drums, made it worth it. At the time Yamaha was tops in offering global support. They also did some promotion which (of course) is always nice.

I left Yamaha somewhat abruptly, my main contact with Yamaha was a man known as "Hagi." He had left Yamaha, and things had changed. The newer people were not very kind when I expressed my interest in lighter flat based hardware, so I impulsively left and went with Drum Workshop. Don Lombardi was very enticing, and the fact that the company was close-by was very appealing. They supported my desire for a flat-based and lightweight cymbal stand that was like my old flat based Ludwig stands (their stands were the closest thing at the time.) But a few things happened that told me that I was not a very good fit with DW.

I started buying a lot of vintage drums while I was with them. I bought some old Rogers and Slingerland kits because I was looking for "something" that I wasn't getting from my DW drums. No one was more surprised than me, when I found "that" in Tama drums. I had always associated them with rock and roll. But I happened into their booth at the NAMM show with a student of mine because he was interested in their drums. Tama respected my relationship with DW, but they asked me to check out their new Tama Star kits. I agreed to have a five drum set shootout that my cartage people helped with. We set up my DW kit, a Sakae kit, a Gretsch kit, and two of the new Tama Star kits all side by side. I played them all and was really impressed with the Tama's. I was impressed enough to take a set to a little gig in the Valley. I also asked my wife to come down and listen to the band and the drums. On the break, she told me that she really liked the way the drums were making me play, and that was it! The company was very helpful, and truthfully, I think I missed the "attitude" of a Japanese drum company.

Professional drummers are like any other drummer. We get turned on by the sound, the look, and the feel of equipment. My only request to Tama was that they promised to collaborate with me to create a flat based cymbal stand that was as close as possible to my old Ludwig flat based stands. There would be no royalties, but I wanted the final approval. They met my requests, and we nailed it! Through the process, they provided the standard of quality and communication that Japanese companies always seem to provide.

I know my timing of leaving DW was very bad. They had just started to promote a "Frequent Flyer" drum set that we had been designing for three years, and it was a very good sounding set. One of the reasons it sounded

Courtesy Tama Drums

so good for an economical kit was because we chose smaller lug casings (versus the larger round/signature DW lugs.) In my time there, they were very generous, and I have the utmost respect for Don Lombardi, but when I left, I returned most every drum that they had sent me.

I have now been with Tama for about seven years, and we have a great relationship. We have a signature snare drum coming out, it's a 4.5" spruce and maple shell, stick saver hoops, made in Japan, eight lugs, with light hardware. We went with four and a half inches, because if we did four, we would have had to use a strainer that I didn't like. So the extra half inch allowed us to use my favorite strainer. It has a reinforcement ring on the batter side, but not on the bottom. That makes the bottom head open up a bit while the top head stays very focused.

We went through about 10 prototype drums before we came up with this exact drum. But we came up with the philosophy of this drum pretty quickly. It is an astonishingly responsive drum, and it is a wonderful jazz snare drum. Simon Philips has one of the prototypes and one of his bandmates told me that Simon hasn't stopped playing it!

MD: Since you brought up your new snare drum, and it is a 4.5" drum. I have to tell you that you and Roy Haynes are pretty responsible for me falling in love with that size drum. For me, it started with the Ludwig 4" Downbeat snare from the 1950's that Roy used. Then there was your Yamaha signature 4" snare in the 90's. I have them both and love them. It has also made me buy a *few* other 4" snares along the way.

Peter: You can blame Max Roach too. His 4x14 Gretsch signature snare drum was fantastic, and I jumped at getting one of those back in the day. My Yamaha drum was their first signature snare drum, and it was a limited-edition drum. We worked for a long time on that drum.

I will openly admit that my life would have been much simpler if I had not have been so impulsive in leaving Yamaha. We did some great stuff together. I was one of the instigators of their Oak drums. I had bought a 7x13 Craviotto Oak drum that I fell in love with. And I told Hagi that they should check out Oak. The next thing I knew they had the Oak Customs. It has been a complicated journey, but things happen for a reason.

MD: I've got a few Yamaha snares, I love the Bamboo drum, it's really close to my Brady Jarrah ply drum.

Peter: I was told that the reason that those bamboo drums sounded so good was because of the amount of epoxy polymer that they used to finish that drum. I also heard that Bamboo was hard to work with. I sold a first-generation copper Roy Haynes drum that I shouldn't have sold, that was a great drum.

MD: I have an older Yamaha Copper Symphonic Concert Snare with the same strainer as was on your signature drum, and I LOVE that drum.

Peter: We did some good stuff together. I suggested to Yamaha to try and figure out the locking nut on the bottom of the hi hat clutch. Hagi told me that one of his friends in Yamaha's motorcycle division helped the drum division come up with a bunch of the new ideas and the solutions to many of the typical drum problems, like my complaint about the hi hat clutch that wouldn't stay tight on the bottom.

MD: I will tell you that the drums on your newest CD entitled *3 Nights in L.A.* are some of the best sounding drums that I have heard on record in a long time.

Peter: Those are the new Tama Star drums, recorded with two Sony overheads, a 57 on the snare, and a Shure SM 7 on the bass drum. That's my favorite record, we didn't rehearse, and for a few of the tunes, George Garzone was just stomping off standards. I feel like I have finally gotten command and control of the instrument, and that is represented on this recording. My ideas and touch are finally to where I'm happy with them. Not in a clinical sense, because I think that I'm playing with enough abandon, and leave enough things to chance. But the physics of my playing are making better sense now. I am matching my abilities to my sonic expectations, and the new drums are helping that.

My Tama's are like a cross between an old Rogers and an old Slingerland kit. I played Slingerland for a long time too. And those were the brands of vintage drums that I sought out when I went on my recent vintage drum buying spree. I played my vintage Rogers kit on the soundtrack to *Mank,* and I recorded the drums here in my studio with some wonderful vintage mics.

When I was a kid, my first drum set was a round badge Gretsch kit. But the first set that I really became obsessed with and wanted to buy, was a natural Ludwig set like Roy Haynes had in the Ludwig ads with Gary Burton. I got that set from Irv's Music in Atlantic City NJ, it was a blond maple kit in 20, 12, 14. I played that set with my Rogers Dynasonic snare for a while. During that time, (believe me) I obsessed over many other drum sets too. I devoured the drum catalogs of Rogers, Sonor, and Ludwig. I had already had a Gretsch kit, so I had already "been there," and I didn't pay too much

Peter's Picks

Sticks: I have had 3 Vic Firth Signature sticks, the Big Band stick is my main choice today, but I like the way the ride stick sounds. I also pushed Vic Firth with the Wood Shaft Bass Drum Beater.

Heads: are usually Remo Coated Ambassadors, if I need more low-end the bass drums get Power Strokes. I like the new Fiberskyns too.

Mic's: I use Shure 98's for toms. I have a Shure SM 7 on the bass drum, and if I need more low end I'll use a Beta 52. My overheads are Sony 1000's, and I like DPA overheads too.

Recording: My interface here at home is a Universal Audio, I've got some Neve Stereo Mic Pre's and some API's as well.

Software: I use Pro-Tools, Logic, and Luna software. I use Sibelius to write, but I am learning Dorico which seems pretty great, and I still use Finale a bit.

Signature Drum Products / Designs:
Yamaha 4x14" Signature Snare Drum Birch (discontinued)
Yamaha FreeStanding StickBag (discontinued)
Yamaha 4x12" Soprano Snare Drum (discontinued)
Yamaha 4x10" Sopranino Snare Drum (discontinued)
Zildjian Left Side Ride (20" + 22")
Zildjian Flash Splash (8" + 10")
Vic Firth SPE1 signature stick
Vic Firth SPE2 "Ride Stick"
Vic Firth SPE3 "Big Band Stick"
Vic Firth "VicKick" VKB5 wood shaft bass drum beater
DW "StandAlone" Stickbag (discontinued)
DW "Frequent Flyer" Drumset (discontinued)
Tama 6.5x10" Signature "Mezzo" stave-shell snare drum
Tama 4.5x14" Signature "Jazz" snare drum (spruce and maple)

Plus numerous contributions to various design improvements made by the Slingerland, Yamaha, Oberheim, DW, Zildjian, Evans, Vic Firth, Shure and Zoom companies over the years.

Comprehensive list of company associations over the years:
Evans Drum Heads, Slingerland Drums, Zildjian Cymbals, Elektrek Microphones, Star Synare Electronic Drums, Yamaha Drums, Remo Drumheads, Oberheim (DMX), Latin Percussion, Simmons Drums, Korg Synthesizers, Beyer Dynamic, Passport Software, KAT Electronics, ddrum, Mark +, Shure Brothers Microphones, Drum Workshop, Tama Drums, Meinl Percussion, Hard Case, various music composing and notation software, various sample libraries, various accessory items, Zoom

attention to Slingerland at first, until I joined the Kenton band.

With Tama I am using the Star drums and I also have a few sets of the Starclassic sets that sound great. I use the Tama "Neo Mod" drums, that have a shallow 10" deep bass drum when I'm schlepping drums around town. I love my Tama drums. My latest obsession is a 14x24 bass drum that I use for period music. Wow … what a sound.

MD: You have helped design many cymbals during your 50 years with Zildjian, let's talk cymbals.

Peter: I'm proud of my long-standing 50-year association with Zildjian, and I've played them for 60 years. My tried and true, go-to ride is my 22" Medium Constantinople, my left side preferences are my 19" Avedis or my 19" K Constantinople. I like to have three rivets in my left side cymbal.

MD: Aren't 19" cymbals just perfect?

Peter: I also use my 20" Left Side ride too. That cymbal was a result of my (like everyone else's) flirtation with boutique cymbals. But I found that all (or most) of the boutique cymbals don't project very well. I like complexity, I like sustain but they have to project.

I have a swish knocker with 20 rivets, and an 18" K sweet crash. Although Zildjian makes a bunch of great hi hats, I always come back to 14" New Beats, they just do everything. I also helped design the new Flash Splashes. I told Zildjian that I wanted a splash that sounded dangerous. Their splashes were sounding too "nice." I also use Meinl percussion.

MD: Were you aware that your Vic Firth signature Ride stick became "the stick" to test cymbals.

Peter: My original stick was the third signature stick that Vic Firth released after Steve Gadd's and Harvey Mason's. That stick was helpful for me (at the time) because the uniformity of the small round ball tip, at the time I was redefining the way that I was setting up, and how hard I was playing my cymbals. But after a while the tip or shoulder got a bit bigger, and the balance was no longer there for me.

The Ride stick was a result of me getting away from the original signature stick. I carried a pair of them around many trade shows playing different cymbals, because all of the sticks that they had at booth's were either nylon tipped, or just too big. There was too much wood and you couldn't hear the sound of the cymbal. That stick evolved into the Big Band stick that Vic Firth makes (and I use) today.

A while back I was thinking of profusely thanking all of the companies that I have (or am) working with, and just use a mishmash of whatever I wanted. Life is short, everyone should play what they want, right? But the practicality of having a company that can offer support anywhere in the world is very nice to have. So, nah! My son once said to me, "Dad … you're Zildjian for life." Of course, I have played Zildjian for my children's entire lives, so why would I ever change? All things considered, I am feeling very fortunate, grateful, and happy to be where I am right now.

Peter and Weather Report

Shigeru Uchiyama

Shigeru Uchiyama

Photo by Jaco Pastorius

Peter and Weather Report

Backstage passes from Weather Reports Hannover and Oslo shows September 1978

Postcard Jaco sent to Peter's mom during his first tour with Weather Report

Ticket from the 1980 Viena show

Courtesy The Peter Erskine Library

Shigeru Uchiyama

Weather Report's 1978 Japan Tour Wayne, Peter, Jaco, Joe.

Shigeru Uchiyama

Peter and Weather Report

All photos on this page by Shigeru Uchiyama

Peter Erskine

Peter Erskine Library

Peter and Weather Report

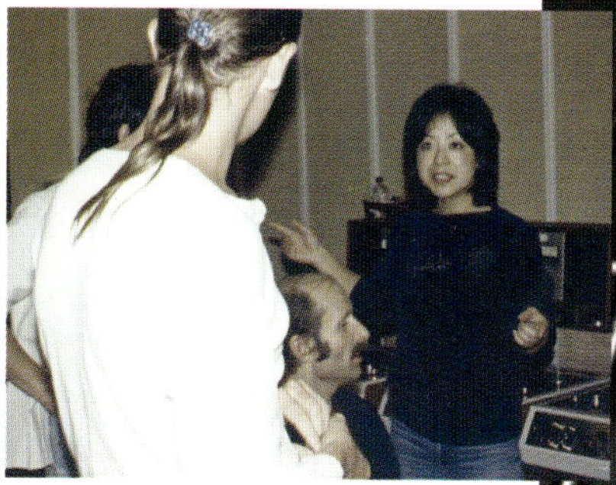

All photos this page Peter Erskine Library

Peter: The Early Years

Peter at the Pleasantville Music Shoppe in Pleasantville, New Jersey circa 1960

Oliver Nelson and Peter circa 1965

Peter: The Early Years photos courtesy Peter Erskine Library

Peter and Friends

1

2

3

4

5

6

7

8

9

1. Rick Latham, Peter, Liberty DeVitto, Horacio "El Negro" Hernandez, Zoro, Wil Kennedy, and Tommy Igoe
2. James Gadson and Peter
3. Lewis Nash, Kenny Washington and Peter
4. Peter and Doudou N'Diaye Rose
5. Vic Firth and Peter
6. Ron Carter and Peter
7. Chick Corea and Peter
8. Mike Clark and Peter
9. Peter and Billy Cobham
10. Alex Acuña, Steve Gadd, and Peter
11. Neil Peart and Peter
12. Jack DeJohnette and Peter
13. Ernie Watts and Peter
14. Chester Thompson, Skip Hadden, Leon Ndugu Chancler, Alex Acuña Omar Hakim, and Peter

Peter and Friends photos courtesy Peter Erskine Library

Peter and Friends

15. Vinnie Colaiuta, Peter, Bobby Colomby and Will Lee behind Vinnie
16. Peter and Airto Moreira
17. Peter and Dennis Chamber
18. Christian McBride and Peter
19. Randy Brecker and Peter
20. Peter, Kenny Aronoff and Jeff Hamilton
21. Dizzy Gillespie and Mutsy Erskine
22. Joe LaBarbera and Peter
23. Elvin Jones and Peter

Peter and Friends photos courtesy Peter Erskine Library

24. Peter and Bob Mintzer
25. Marc Johnson, Eliane Elias, Peter and Mike Mainieri
26. Peter and Don Alias
27. Jim Keltner and Peter
28. The Sweet Soul Band
29. Peter and Jack DeJohnette
30. Peter's daughter Maya and Vic Firth
31. John Abercrombie and Peter
32. Pat Williams and Peter
33. Peter and John DeChristopher
34. The Seth MacFarlane rhythm section
35. Freddie Hubbard All Stars

Peter and Friends photos courtesy Peter Erskine Library

Peter and Family

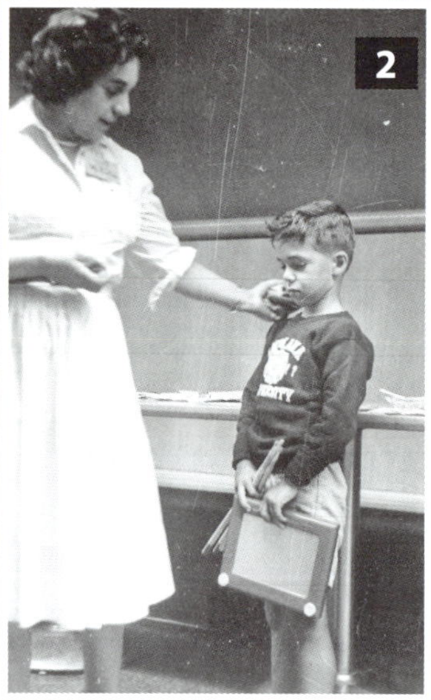

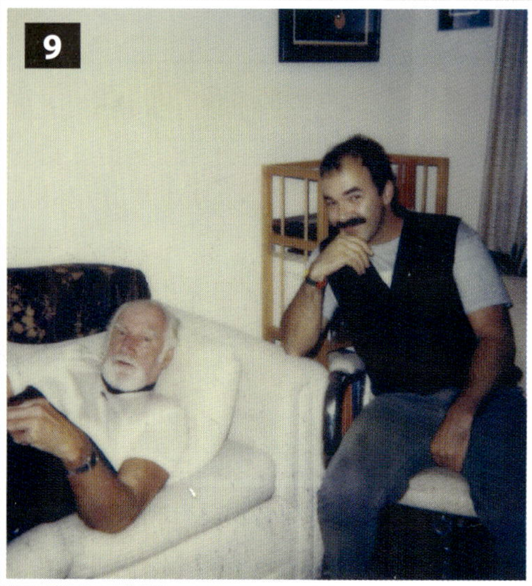

1. Peter's father Fred Erskine M.D. and Peter
2. Peter's Mom Lois, and Peter 1961
3 The Erskines; Peter, son Taichi, Mutsy, and daughter Maya.
4. Dr. Fred and Lois Erskine
5. Dr. Fred Erskine
6. Peter and Mutsy At the Grammys
7. The Erskine's Christmas photo
8. Mutsy Erskine
9. Dr. Fred and Peter
10. Taichi, Mutsy, Maya, and Peter
11. The Erskines in Viena
12. The Erskines; Peter recieved The USC Associates Award For Artistic Expression, 2015
13, The Erskines in Paris
14. Mutsy and Peter
15. Maya, Peter and Taichi carving a pumpkin for Halloween
16. Mutsy and Peter
17. The Erskines at a NAMM show
18.Peter and Mutsy

Peter and family photos courtesy Peter Erskine Library

WEATHER REPORT
THE LEGENDARY LIVE TAPES: 1978-1981

Sweet Soul
PETER ERSKINE

THE SONGS

STEPS AHEAD

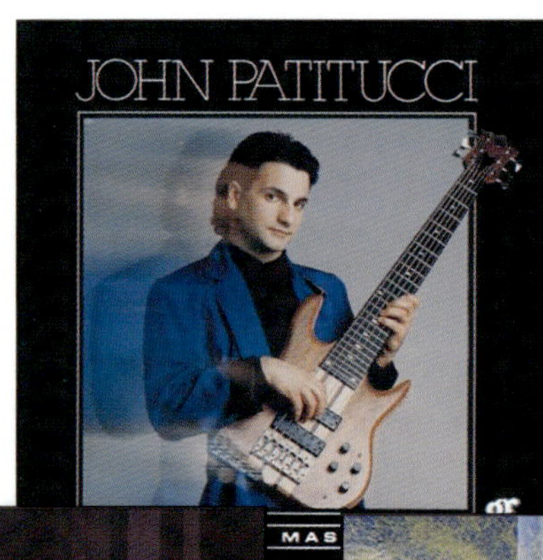
JOHN PATITUCCI

Jaco Pastorius
Word of Mouth

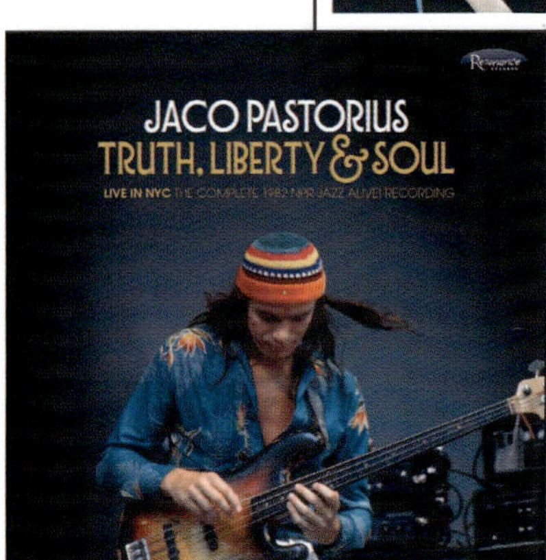
JACO PASTORIUS
TRUTH, LIBERTY & SOUL
LIVE IN NYC THE COMPLETE 1982 NPR JAZZ ALIVE! RECORDING

START HERE
VINCE MENDOZA

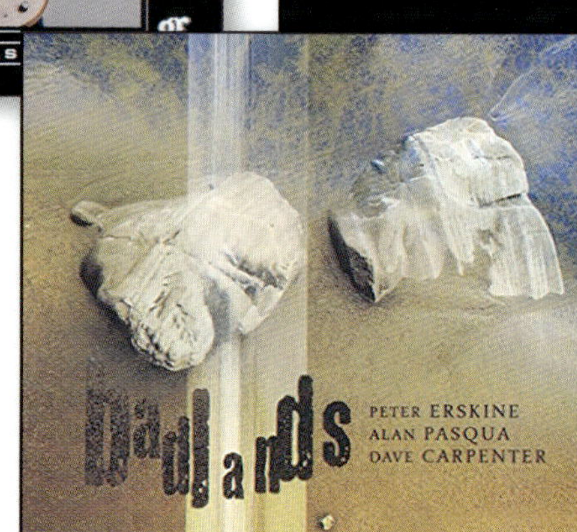
badlands
PETER ERSKINE
ALAN PASQUA
DAVE CARPENTER

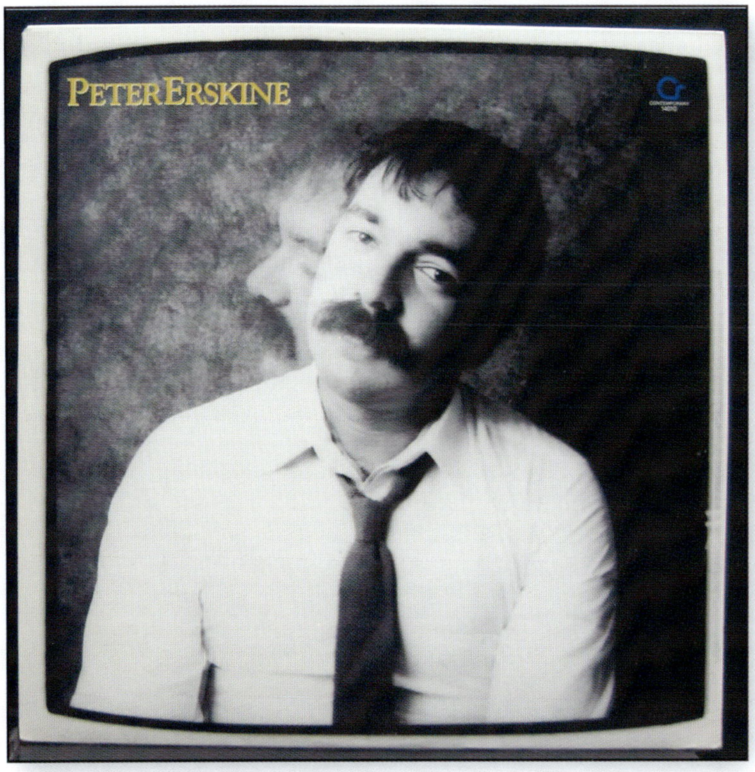
PETER ERSKINE

KENNY WHEELER
MUSIC FOR LARGE & SMALL ENSEMBLES
ECM

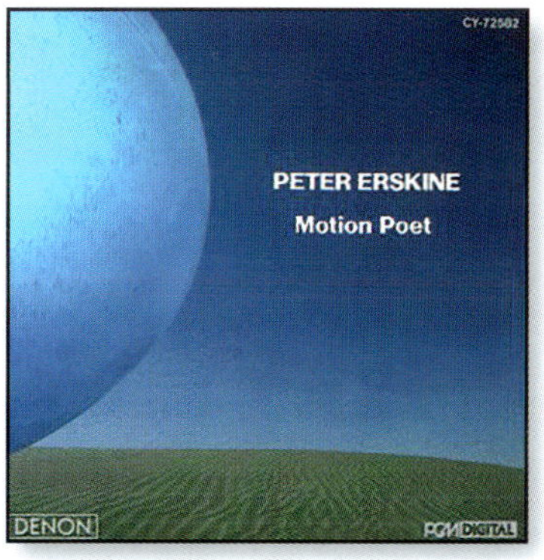
PETER ERSKINE
Motion Poet
DENON

RANDY BRECKER
w/MICHAEL BRECKER
SOME SKUNK FUNK

BOB MINTZER
ALL L.A. BAND

MUSIC FOR MODERNS
STEREO
FEATURING
THE LOUNGE ART ENSEMBLE
BOB SHEPPARD • DAVE CARPENTER • PETER ERSKINE

Marc Johnson Bass Desires Bill Frisell John Scofield Peter Erskine

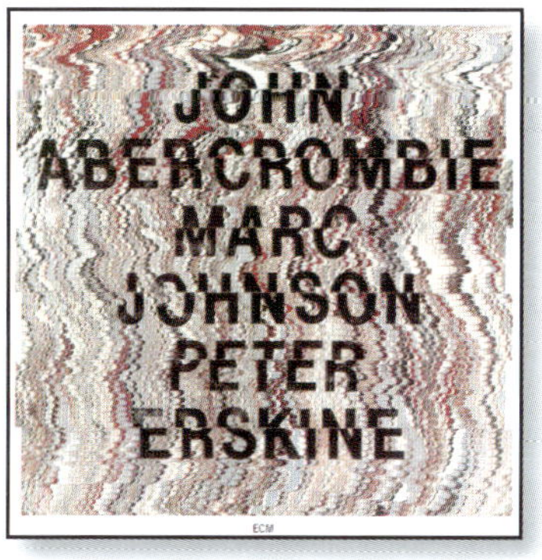
JOHN ABERCROMBIE
MARC JOHNSON
PETER ERSKINE

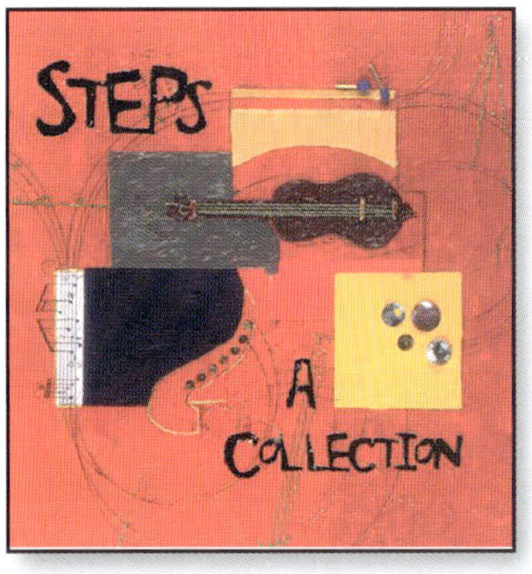
STEPS
A COLLECTION

BOB BERG
DENON

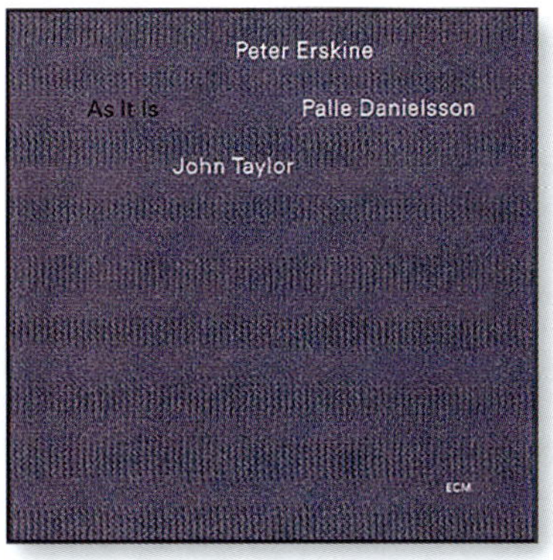
Peter Erskine
As It Is
Palle Danielsson
John Taylor
ECM

PETER ERSKINE is DR. UM
AND... the LOST PAGES
co-starring
JOHN BEASLEY · JANEK GWIZDALA
featuring
BOB SHEPPARD and JEFF PARKER
with LARRY KOONSE and AARON SERFATY

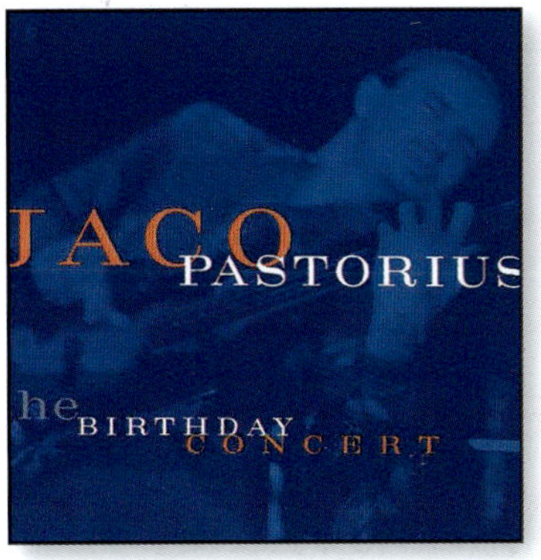
JACO PASTORIUS
The BIRTHDAY CONCERT

Transcriptions

By Terry Branam

Peter's Thoughts on...

By Mark Griffith

Peter Erskine's quintessential playing appears on over 600 albums in various settings, both as a sideman and a leader. Peter's drumming style is gracefully understated, full of life and brimming with class. His masterful control and lightness of touch coax rich tones from his drums and delicate shades of color from his cymbals. He is just as capable of playing dense waves of notes as he is likely to not play anything at all depending on what the music calls for. Erskine has rightfully earned a place as an elder statesman of our instrument, and continues to burn brightly as one of the greats of our time.

MUSIC KEY

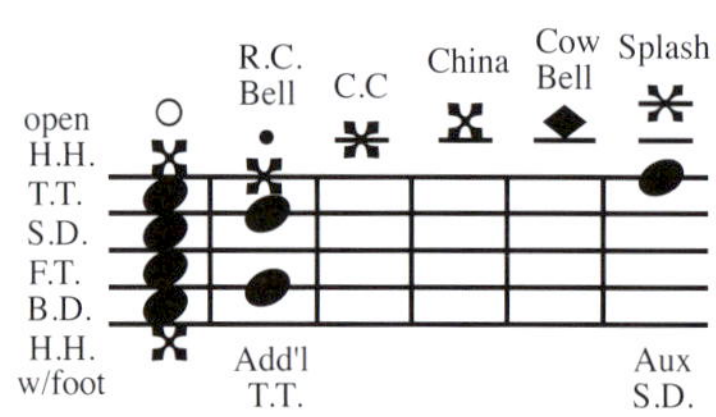

"Black Market," Weather Report, *The Legendary Live Tapes*

Ex 1 - Peter lays down a signature groove on the A section of Weather Report's "Black Market. He plays the last three sixteenths on the ride bell while anchoring the time with quarter notes on the bass drum and backbeats on the snare drum. (1:34)

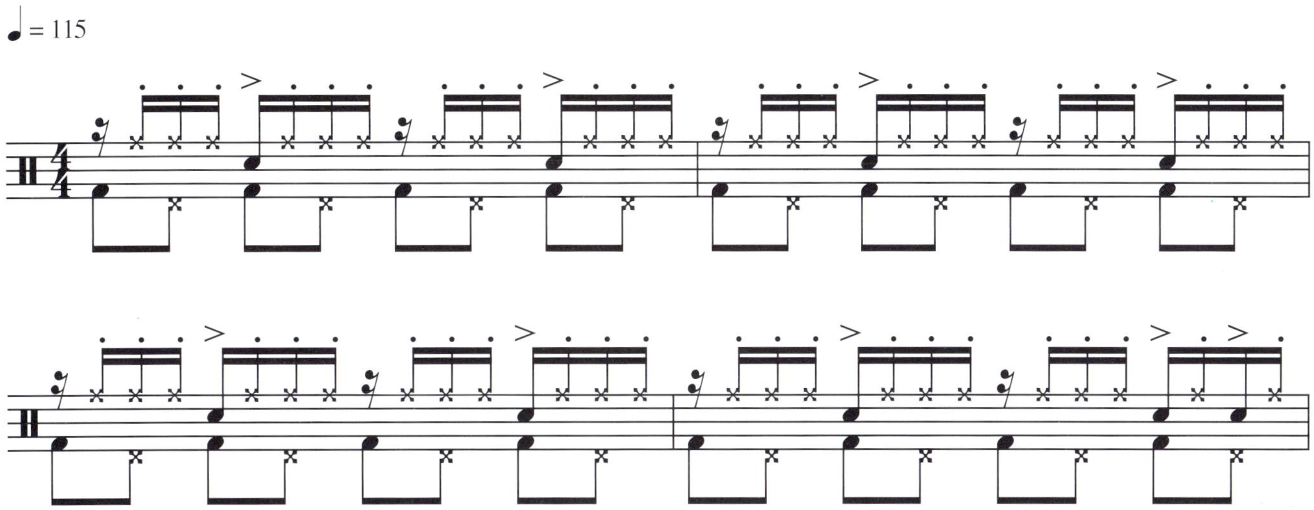

Ex 2 - Erskine accompanies Wayne Shorter's solo with a samba batucada feel. He embellishes the groove with drags on the snare drum and floor tom accents on beats 2 and 4. (5:08)

Peter's Thoughts on...

"Black Market," Weather Report, The Legendary Live Tapes

I'm very proud that there is a cymbal beat in this tune that is pretty unique. Billy Cobham took Vernell Fournier's "Poinciana" off-beat &'s and perfected them into a high- powered fusion groove. So I took that, and added the "a" and sometimes the e&a to it. I first used this on Maynard Ferguson recording

of Earth Wind & Fire's tune "Fantasy." I used it again here on the tune "Black Market." That groove may be my one claim to a signature beat. That song was also the beginning of learning about drum counterpoint, and not resorting to mimicry when accompanying a soloist

"Peter's Solo," - Weather Report, *The Legendary Live Tapes*

Ex 3 - The opening statement of "Peters Solo" revolves around a 3:2 rhumba clave rhythm voiced around the kit. He ends the phrase with choked crash cymbals and snare drum accents. (0:02)

"Peter's Drum Solo (Osaka 1978)," - Weather Report, *The Legendary Live Tapes*

Ex 4 - Erskine's stream-of-consciousness soloing approach is at work on the Osaka 1978 drum solo. He flies around the drums connecting ideas with triplets between the hands and feet.

B

C

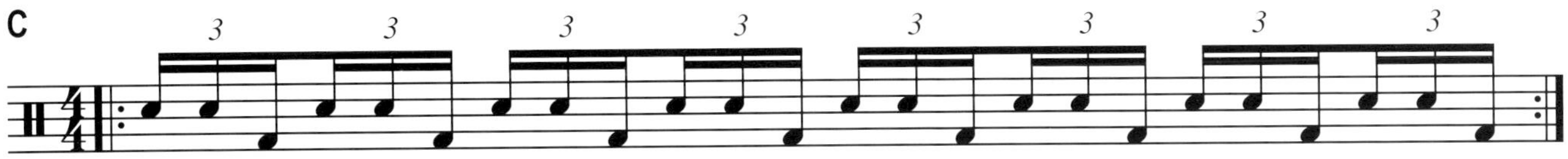

D

Ex 5 - Here are some more examples of Peter's phrasing within this solo:

A

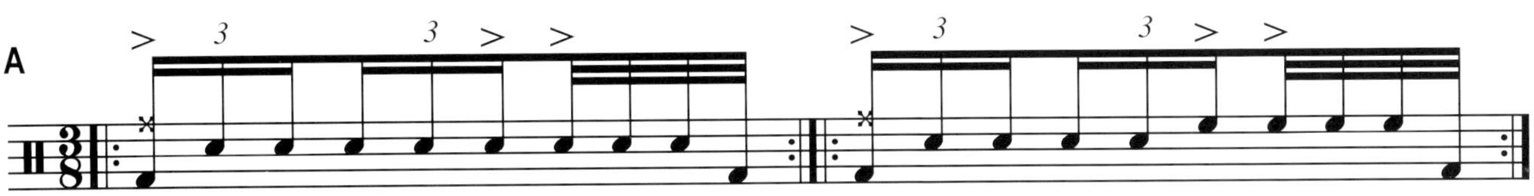

B

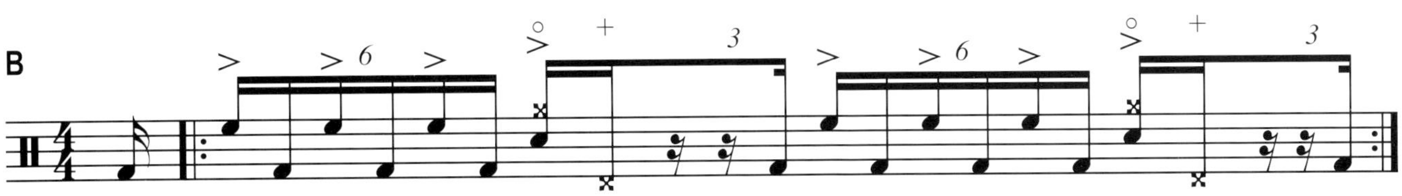

C

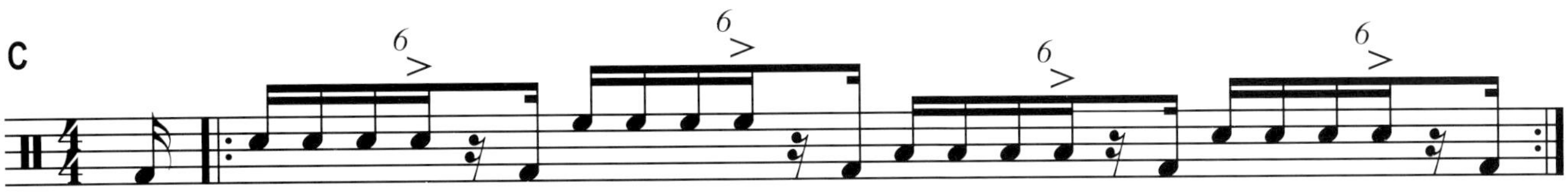

D

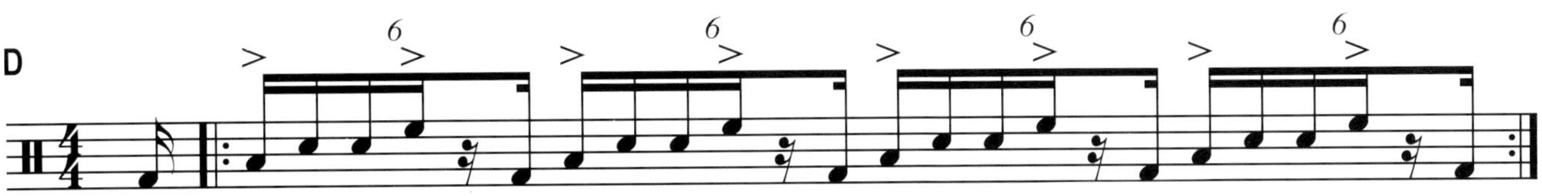

E

Peter's Thoughts on…
"Drum Solo," (there are two,)
Weather Report, *The Legendary Live Tapes*

I am surprised by my lack of modesty that I even included those solos on the Weather Report set that I recently produced. Upon listening to this now, I'll give it an A for effort! My single strokes were in pretty good shape back in those days. And, like most drum solos, this came along well into the concert. One of these solos was recorded during the USA tour as part of the "live" 8:30 album recording. Are drum solos daunting moments or welcome opportunities? Maybe a combination of the two, I suppose. Listening now, I wish I had chosen to play shorter solos. Compositionally, these are "searching" more than "finding!" But that stopped cymbal and bass drum thing near the beginning of the solo is worth the price of admission.

The other solo is from my 2nd or 3rd night with the band during my first tour with the group in Japan. I can hear where I'm doing my best to "get" to the worlds of Elvin Jones or Eric Gravatt, but with a 22" bass drum and toms with black dot heads. The Japan tour solo is more akin to the Steps "Paradox/Aleph" solo than the "8:30" era solo. In both solos, I can hear a sense of my playing to some sort of undefined expectation. I can hear the tension between artistic honesty and my trying to get some "wows" from the audience (if not Wayne, Joe and Jaco!)

All of that said, the solo in Osaka that leads into 'Directions" is not bad. And when Wayne comes in with "Directions," wow! Imagine what this might have sounded like if only I'd been playing on a 4-piece kit with an 18" bass drum!

"Fast City," Weather Report, *The Legendary Live Tapes*

Ex 6 - Erskine handles the brisk tempo of "Fast City" with an intricate funk groove. (0:59)
**note: written in half-time for clarity*

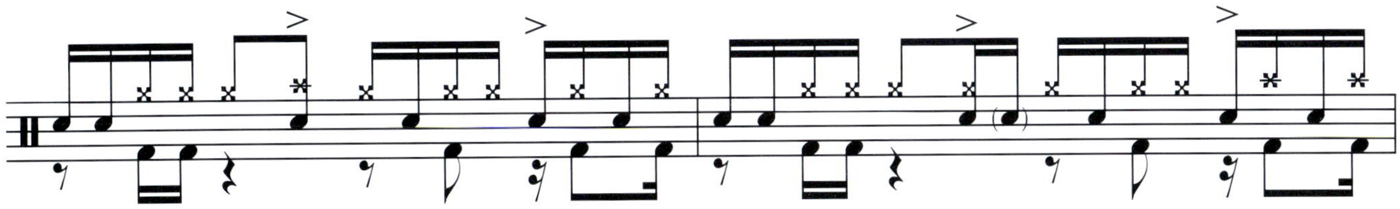

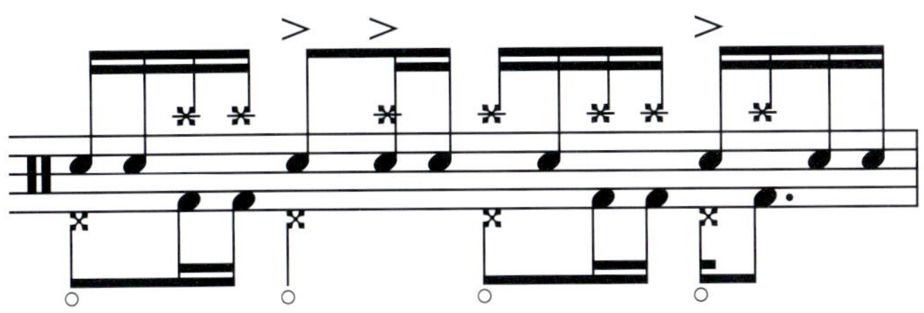

Peter's Thoughts on…
"Fast City," Weather Report, *The Legendary Live Tapes*

Very fast. That was a wild tune. I felt challenged to come up with something that maybe Eric Gravatt or Ishmael Wilburn might have played. Like Ishmael's beat on "Nubian Sundance" from *Mysterious Traveler*. That beat was my "audition" for Weather Report.

What happened was that Zawinul called me up first, and our conversation seemed very inconclusive. So he had a manager call me and ask me if I could play the beat from "Nubian Sundance." We used to play that tune as our soundcheck In Maynard's band. So I replied, "Yeah you tell Joe that I can play the shit out of it." Zawinul loved that answer, so they flew me out for a live audition. It's an insanely complicated beat. So the "Fast City" beat was a variation of that beat.

"Sightseeing," Weather Report, *The Legendary Live Tapes*

Ex. 7 -Wayne Shorter's "Sightseeing" is an angular uptempo bop tune with lots of rhythmic twists and turns. Peter navigates the head of the song by accentuating key points of the melody on the drums and adding statements in the spaces. (0:00)

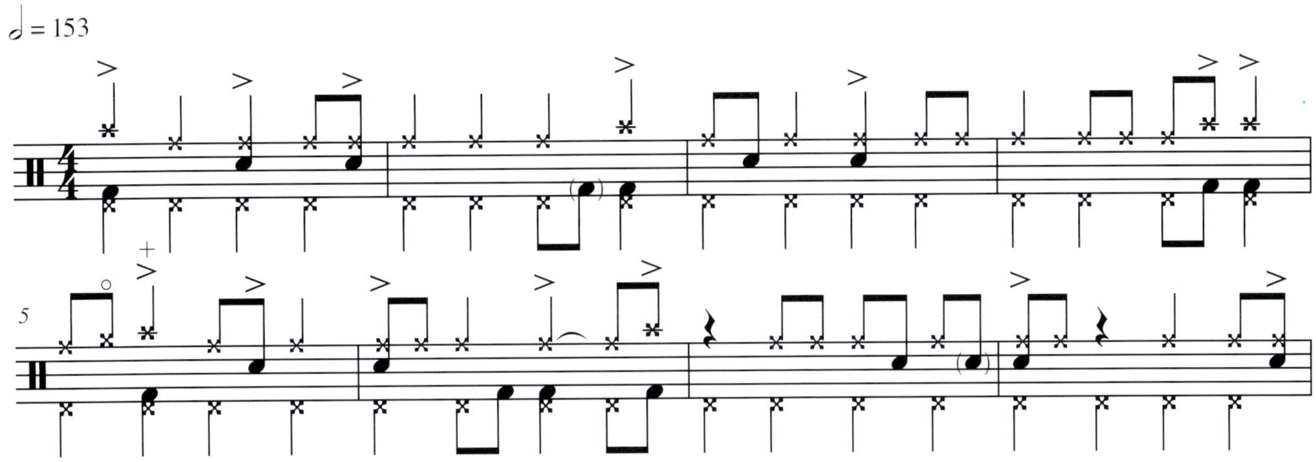

Peter's Thoughts on…

"Sightseeing," Weather Report, *The Legendary Live Tapes*

That's a good one, I like that. After we originally recorded that tune, we realized that it needed to go somewhere else. So we came up with the interlude that you hear on this live version. I was still thinking of Eric and Ishmael on "Nubian Sundance" for this as well. I was wondering what those guys would play. I was also being influenced by what Jaco called his "Florida Beat" (as can be heard on "Teen Town.")

The 4/4 on the hi hat was an obvious Tony thing, but (surprisingly) my single strokes sound really good on this, and they are really effective. That was a device that I ultimately left behind, but I thought that what I played on this tune would stand the test of time. And I think it did.

"Pools," Steps Ahead, *Steps Ahead*

Ex. 8 - Erskine plays a reggae-inspired groove on the intro of the classic Steps Ahead tune "Pools". The bass drum plays a four-bar pattern that catches a piano accent on the "and" of two on the first measure, then settles into beat three for the remainder of the phrase. (0:00)

Ex 9 - The groove at letter C flips around, and he leads the beat with a left hand cross stick. The right hand flams on the rim of the snare drum. (2:07)

Left hand: x stick
Right hand: snare rim

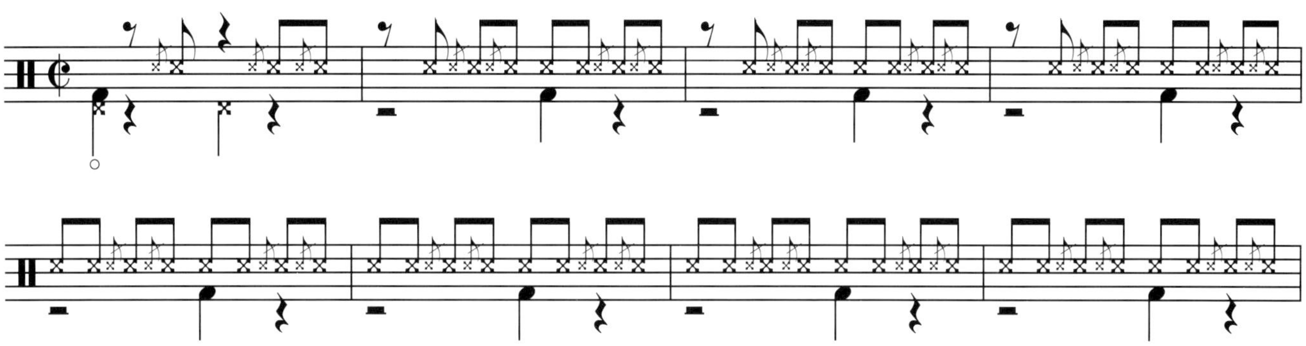

Peter's Thoughts on…
"Pools," Steps Ahead

When I first played this, I played it with eighth notes on the hi hat, a backbeat, and I was catching all the figures. But Don Grolnick (the composer) didn't want that. Instead, I went with what we hear on the record. That groove actually originates with Grady Tate on "Killing Me Softly," and I think he got it sort of sideways from Bernard. Gadd and Chris Parker did that beat a lot too. But it's the

ingenuity of the tune that makes the beat seem more *clever* than it actually is. There is actually something on the interlude to "Pools" that I might be able to lay some claim to. On the right hand I am playing &a1, &a2, &a3, &a4 while I am playing e&a with my left. So I flam them to create that beat. I used to do that flam thing a lot. I don't anymore, I am much more direct now.

"Know Where You Are," Kenny Wheeler, *Music for Small & Large Ensembles*

Ex 10 - Erskine's big band playing often finds him avoiding the conventions of traditional approaches. In this example, he plays accents between the horn figures, providing a unique spin to the section. (1:32)

Ex 11 - He plays an implied duple feel to smoothly transition into the 12/8 groove. (2:45)

Peter's Thoughts on…

"Know Where You Are," Kenny Wheeler, *Music for Large and Small Ensembles*

Kenny Wheeler is one of music's greatest treasures whether he's writing or playing the trumpet. Kenny put together this big band as a celebration of his music for a tour of Great Britain in 1990.

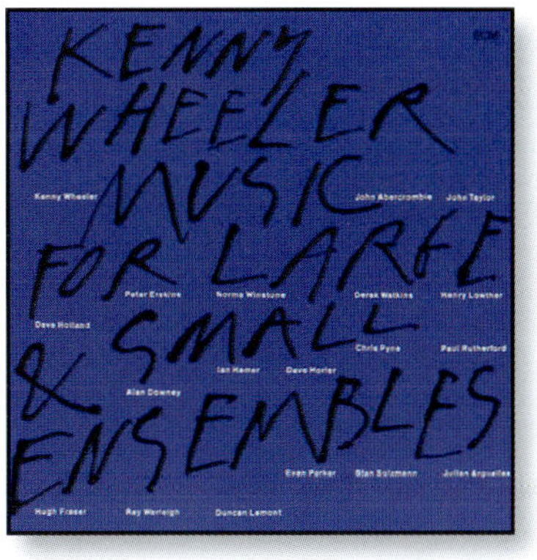

I catch some of the big band figures by setting them up or accenting them while allowing other ones to pass by without comment, sometimes it's refreshing to hear a horn section pop a rhythmic figure without the drums doing so in unison. It can be a cool idea to play the holes or spaces in the arrangement, i.e., play simple accents or figures of your own creation between some of the band's "tutti" statements, you can hear me doing some of that on this track. The tune modulates between 4/4 and ¾. This is a good example of a drum part that is not too specific in terms of when and where to play accents when reading a chart like this your ears are just important as your eyes!

The charts for this tune and more discussion of this song are included in the Peter Erskine book The Drum Perspective by Hal Leonard Publications. halleonard.com

HL # 06620015

"Searching, Finding," John Patitucci, *John Patitucci*

Ex 12 - John Patitucci's composition "Searching, Finding" is a medium-tempo swing tune that features an all-star cast of players. The intro is an open section with ensemble hits on the "and" of beats two and three. Peter fills the space with aggressive playing that takes full advantage of the wide open landscape. (0:00)

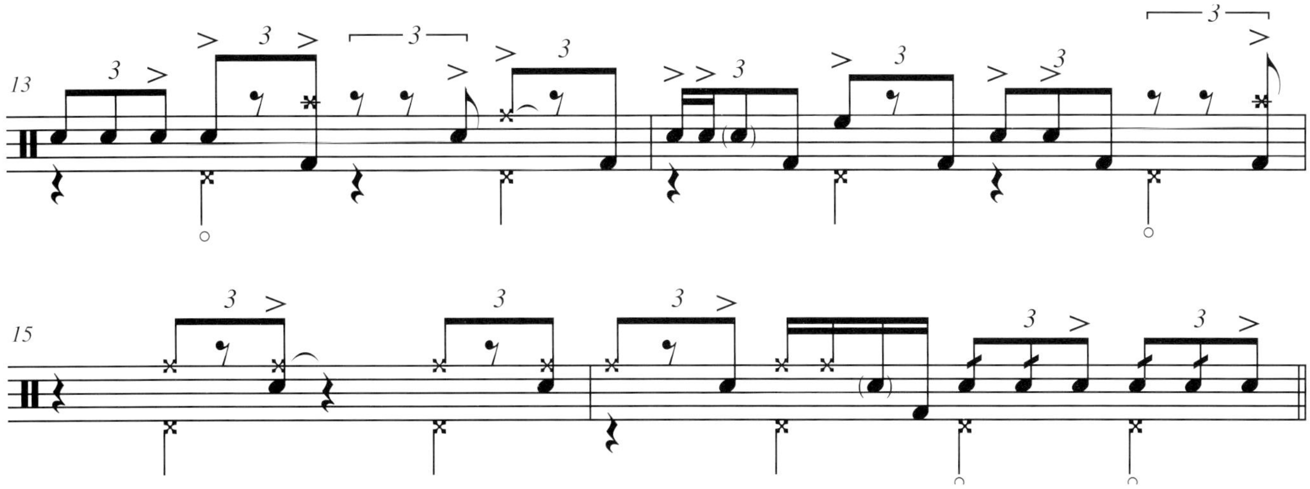

Ex 13 - Peter solos over the figures near the end of the song, interacting with Chick Corea's inventive comping. (4:05)

Peter's Thoughts on…
"Searching, Finding," John Patitucci

That was the second time that I had the opportunity to play with Chick Corea, and much more satisfying than the first one (on Joe Henderson's *Relaxin' At Camarillo*, years earlier.) I borrowed Peter Donald's Yamaha drums, I had just moved to LA. Mike Brecker added his part later. The tune had some nice built-in hits that I could hang my drumming on.

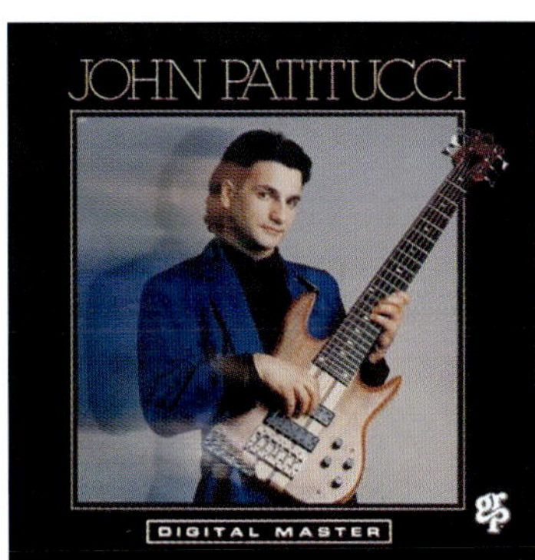

MD: How do you conceive your playing when you are laying down a track for a soloist to overdub on later, I've always had a hard time with that?

Peter: You try to keep your playing relatively transparent. You play some pretty universal ideas, and keep them pretty predictable. If you get too busy you are totally handcuffing the soloist. So you have to figure out a way to dial up the temperature without being too dense. If you play with intention, and compositionally, the soloist can hear where you are going.

"Reza," Jaco Pastorius, *The Birthday Concert*

Ex 14 - Erskine sets up an Afro-Cuban 12/8 groove to back up Othello Molineaux's steel pan solo on the Jaco Pastorius Big Band song "Reza". (3:22)

Ex 15 - He bends the subdivisions at will on this solo break. (7:24)

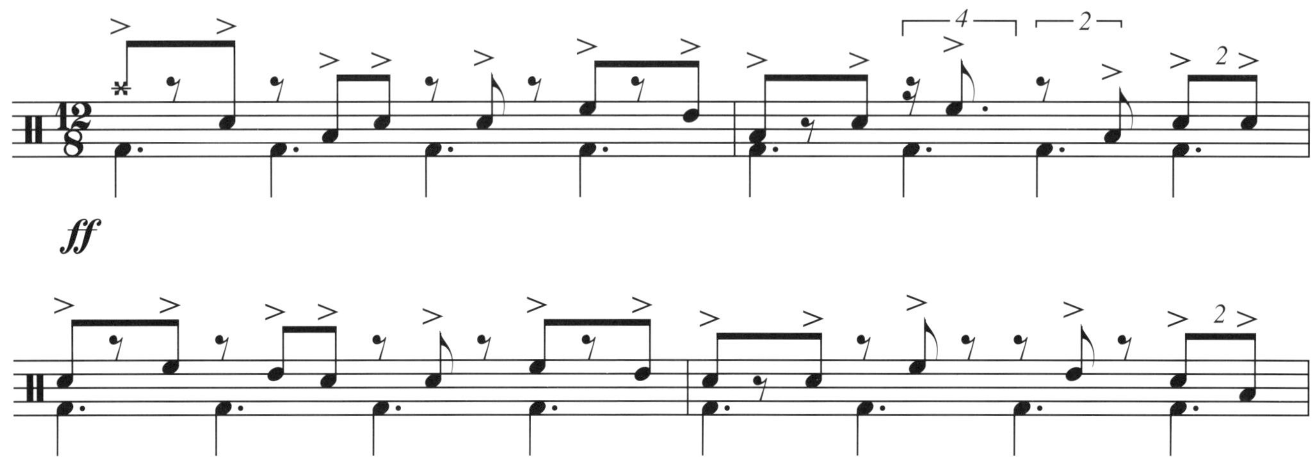

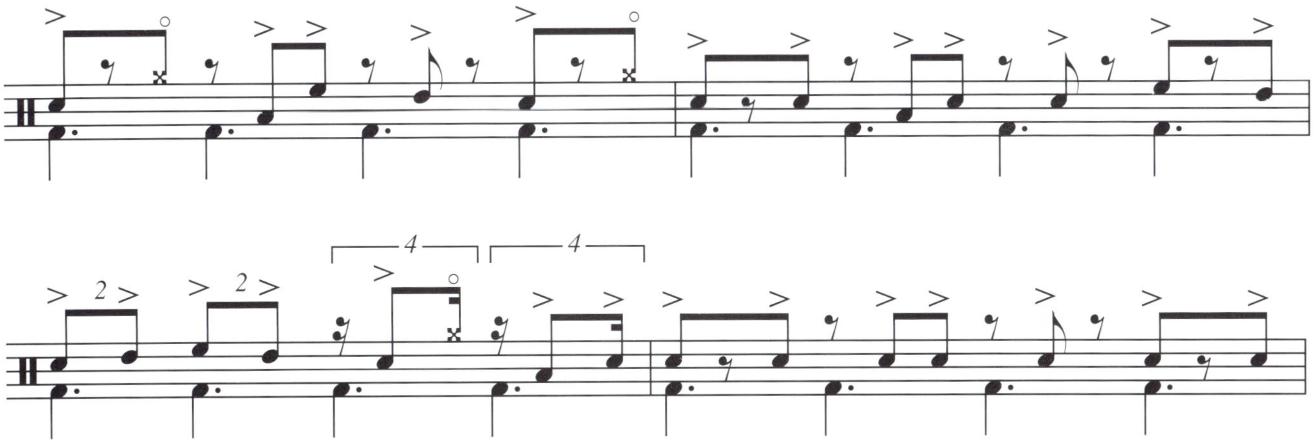

Peter's Thoughts on…
"Reza," Jaco Pastorius, *The Birthday Concert*

That's just a 12/8 groove that was influenced by drummer Chuck Lampkin from Lalo Schifrin's "Gillespiana."

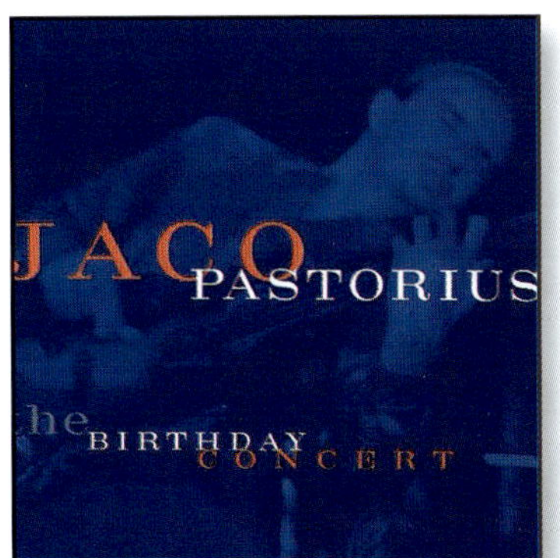

"Liberty City," Jaco Pastorius, *The Birthday Concert*

Ex 16 - Jack DeJohnette plays a lively "one-drop" shuffle on "Liberty City". The left hand cross-stick dances around the bass drum that lands on beat three of the bar. (0:21)

Ex 17 - A crescendoing snare roll sets up the bridge. Jack switches to backbeats on the open hi-hat to give the groove a lift. (3:41)

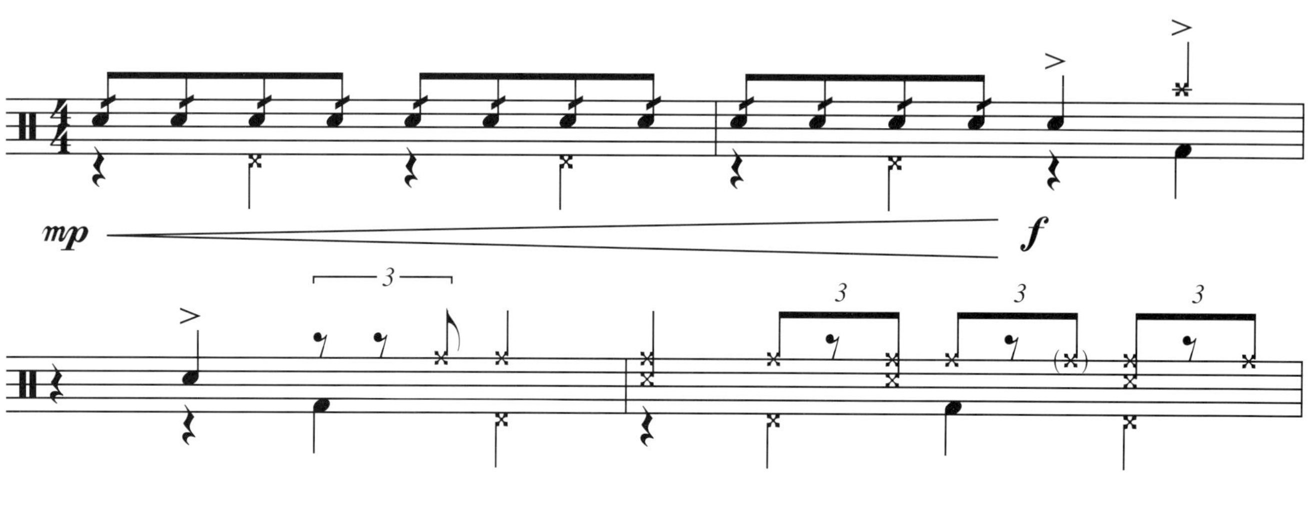

Peter's Thoughts on...
"Liberty City," Jaco Pastorius, Word of Mouth

Actually, this is Jack DeJohnette playing on this track. All of the drummers are listed on the liner notes for the record, but it doesn't break down who is on which tracks, but this is Jack. I played it first at rehearsals, but Jack DeJohnette recorded it on *Word of Mouth*. Jack interpreted whatever I had come up with, and he made it special on the recording. He can do that with anything, Jack is too brilliant for words! Truthfully, I got into Jack DeJohnette before I had gotten into Tony Williams. This was the most fun tune to play with Jaco.

"Ellis Island," Bob Mintzer Big Band, *All L.A. Band*

Ex 18 - The intro of "Ellis Island" starts with a spacious 6/8 groove. He mirrors the band figures on the bass drum, and ties everything together with ghost notes and offbeat hi-hat rhythms. (0:00)

Peter's Thoughts on…

"Ellis Island," Bob Mintzer Big Band, All L.A. Band

I didn't know this tune that well when we recorded it, so this is a fairly conservative version. The band had run down the first 16 bars. Bob stopped us and we did this take, so I'm just basically sight-reading it on the recording. I like the version that I did for the Zildjian demo of the new splashes much more. We included this tune on my play along app.

I did a tune with Bob called "Heart of the Matter," I played really well on that, and there is a solo that I actually like (my kids were in the booth so I was

Ex 19 - When the band arrives at the fortissimo shout chorus, Peter plays with great intensity without adding an excessive amount of notes. (3:47)

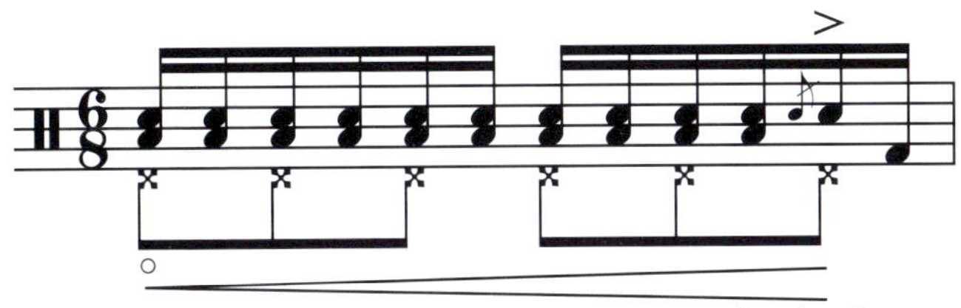

probably just showing off.) On the solo, I soloed on the vamp twice through, and on the third time through I went back to time to let it simmer a bit, then I came back even stronger in on the fourth and final time through the vamp. Sort of like in a horror movie, when you think the villain is knocked down, and

then he pops back to life, and then you finally kill him in the last scene. It makes dramatic sense, that's how I think when I solo.

We did a first version, and the brass needed a second take. So we (in the rhythm section) were sort of imitating ourselves on the second take. But that's some of my favorite playing with Bob.

"Samurai Hee-Haw," Marc Johnson, *Bass Desires*

Ex 20 - Peter establishes the 3/4 groove of "Samurai Hee-Haw" and sets up the melody with a tasteful fill. (0:56)

Ex. 21 -The drums solo over a vamp near the end of the song. Erskine plays with space at the beginning, and utilizes tension and release phrasing as he weaves in and out of different rhythmic subdivisions. He drops down to a whisper near the end and crescendos out of the solo, making a grand exit. (5:48)

9
13
17
21
25
29
33

Peter's Thoughts on…

"Samurai Hee-Haw," Marc Johnson, *Bass Desires*

That's my futile attempt at double time drumming, I get a little embarrassed when I hear that now, it's a good tune though.

"Esperança," Peter Erskine, Palle Danielsson, John Taylor, As it Is

Ex 22 - Erskine's elegant cymbal playing accompanies the melody of "Esperança". (0:00)

Ex 23 - Peter applies a subtle backbeat groove to the 5/4 section. (0:51)

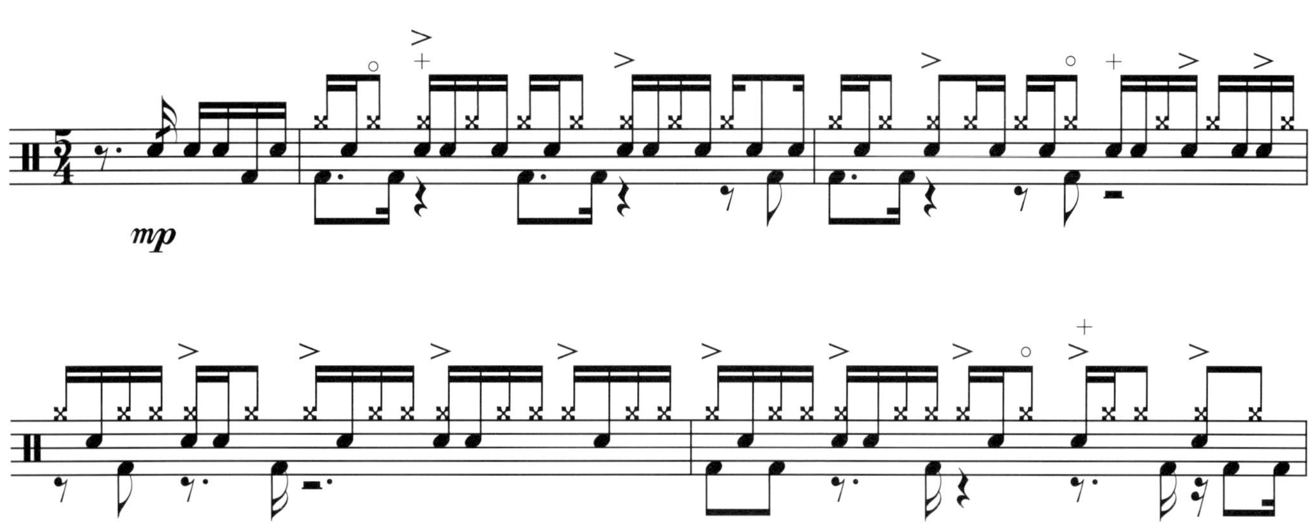

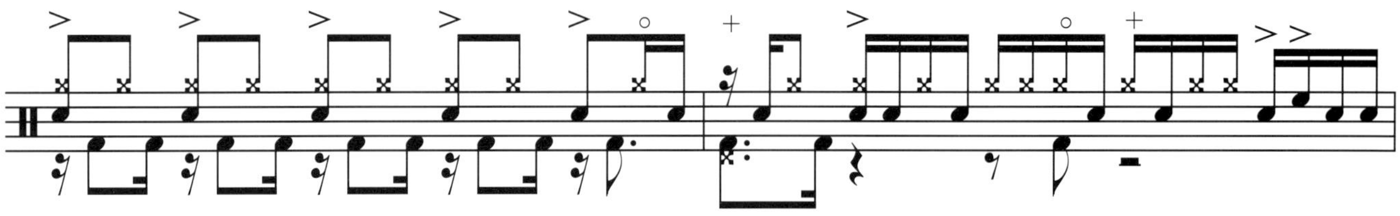

Ex 24 - While the band vamps under his solo, Peter phrases through the 5/4 meter with thirty-second note stickings and snare drum rolls. (2:53)

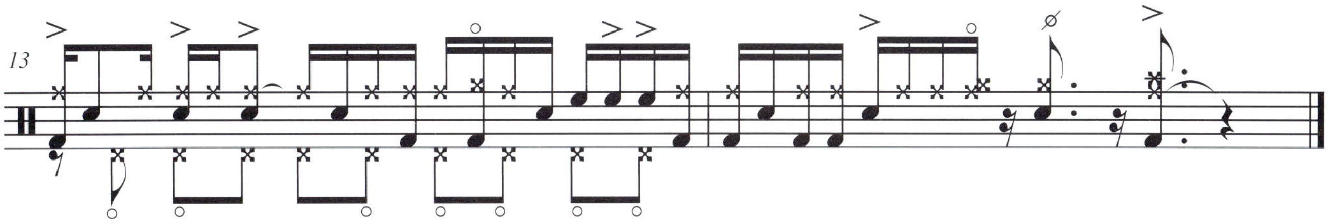

Peter's Thoughts on…
"Esperança," Peter Erskine, *As It Is*

ECM has always provided solace and space for musically intelligent conversations. Manfred Eicher created an esthetic ideal, one that reflects the very nature of good music itself: the quality of TONE, the use of SPACE, an appreciation for BEAUTY, and the balance between SILENCE and NOTES.

In this way, Manfred Eicher was as much of a poet as he was a producer or music business visionary. I am very happy that our orbits intersected for the dozen albums I recorded with him. While recording for ECM as a sideman and a leader, I was able to travel, perform, and record with some amazing musicians. For a working and improvising musician, this is a gift from the gods.

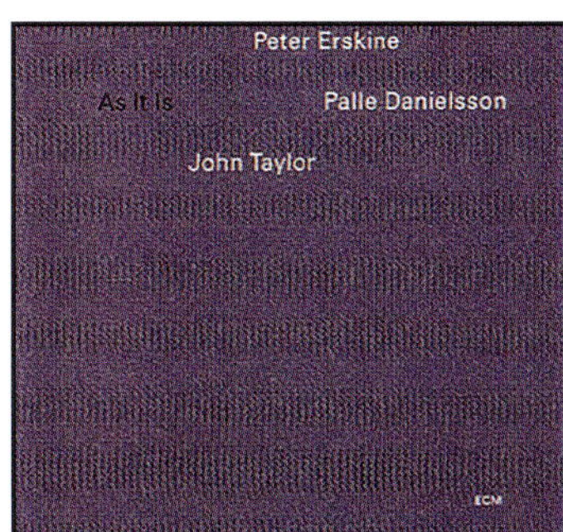

However, if and when I tried to play how I imagined Jack DeJohnette or Jon Christensen might play ECM music, I only ended up sounding like a very bad imitation of one or the other. "To thine own self be true." What I now know is this: whenever I play, the song will always tell me what to do. And, that said, I like and prefer music that swings (or at least dances.)

The greater calling of music (and the muse) provides guidance, inspiration, comfort, as well as an unrelenting demand to be musical. Today, I find this by playing less on the drums, by injecting less of my habits into the music, and by being saved from myself by the grace of silence and space (for however brief those moments might be.) I like music that sparkles with imagination, tone, and nuance. And, in the lovely paradox that is art and self, once I surrender to silence and space, I find much more control in the shaping and destiny of the music. By playing less, I can exert more in terms of the direction and the shape of the music. So, instead of being the puppet, I am ultimately the puppeteer.

Pianist John Taylor was, simply, a brilliant player. I heard him for the first time with Kenny Wheeler and Norma Winstone in their Azimuth trio, and I was like, "Wow!" We were splitting a bill at the Fat Tuesday's jazz club in New York and, normally, when it wasn't your turn to play you'd go outside or to the dressing room and do whatever … but I was just riveted, I had to listen to every set they played. I never heard anyone play like John, so, when I got the chance to work with him and Kenny, I was thrilled.

In Kenny's band, we would do a trio tune as part of the quintet set. That led to the idea of the piano trio that ultimately became John Taylor, Palle Danielsson and myself. At first that trio had the sole purpose of doing my solo album for Manfred Eicher and his ECM label.

Most piano trios are not led by drummers this always led to some confusion. The economics of it were (basically) that my name was easier to book, so for the booking agent and everyone else, it was agreed to bill the trio that way. That said, I also had an aesthetic vision for the group, which was often at odds with their playing energies.

I had spent so much time playing energetically, that I wanted this trio to be my chance to "break on through to the other side," as it were. One of the things that I used to do to these poor guys would be to have a post-mortem talk after most every concert. These after-the-fact discussions about things always started off, "Hey guys, it was great tonight, but … I feel that we're trying to be too energetic or too clever on some of these tunes." These were the types of after-concert notes I would give.

These discussions had to do with not treating every solo or every improvisation like we're in a soccer or football match where every solo represented an opportunity to score a goal. I guess I come from more of a baseball background … where it's good for batters to walk or hit a single, versus trying to hit a home run every time they're at bat. Back to the soccer analogy: "it's okay for us to pass the ball back and forth and keep it in the backfield for a while…"

I brought a tune into the first trio album session that the producer disliked immensely. John was skeptical too. But

I wanted to try this, and in the end (after only one take,) the recording of it came out quite nice, thanks mainly to John and Palle's beautiful playing. But when we would play "On The Lake" live, I would remind them, "Guys, you know, the song is called "On the Lake." We're driving by a lake and there's a bit of mist on the lake, that's all there is to the picture, that's all there is to the story. The Loch Ness monster is not coming out of the lake. A jet aircraft is not crashing into the lake. There's no Russian submarine coming out of the lake or anything else… it's just some mist on the lake and we happen to see it, maybe the way the moonlight is reflecting off it, but that's as far as it goes. I don't want the tune to be about anything else. And for better or worse, that's why it was *my trio.* I think, ultimately, John got tired of that, but I thought we did a good job of exploring that kind of **non-energy energy**.

That's pretty much how I regard that entire four-album relationship-experiment. I learned much from John and Palle. This is a good time to mention that playing in trios is unique because it is a triangle. The weight or responsibility — the lead voice – can move quite freely in any and all directions. The trio dynamic can be the most interesting of group formations, and it can also be one of the most challenging, especially for a drummer… It starts with the name, *The Piano Trio!*

The Bill Evans trio was such an imposing presence. And your choices were: you can either go the Bill route, the Oscar Peterson route, the Keith Jarrett route, or the Red Garland or Wynton Kelly route. None of these seemed to be my thing, it was a vocabulary I didn't feel particularly comfortable or interested in speaking. Even Keith's amazing trio got a bit too athletic for my taste, though looking back, that was an amazing group.

With "my" ECM trio, even though I flex my muscles quite a bit on some of the tunes, I saw that trio vehicle or a doorway to something else. Eventually I was able to realize this more fully with a trio with Alan Pasqua here in Los Angeles. Alan and I just celebrated our 50th anniversary musically. There's a level of trust between us that is pretty astonishing. As you all know, when you trust someone you don't need to tell them as much. It's usually just a little wink or a nod, sometimes it's not even that. It's simply that we tend to know what each other is thinking. Paradoxically, that trio was of no interest to ECM. I don't know why. So the only thing left to do was to start my own record label, Fuzzy Music.

"Cats and Kittens," Lounge Art Ensemble, *Music for Moderns*

Ex 25 - Peter lays down a miniaturized second line groove on a small cocktail drum kit for the Lounge Art Ensemble's "Cats and Kittens". He draws many textures from the snare drum by applying staccato presses, drags, shallow rimshots and accents. (0:00)

Peter's Thoughts on…
"Cats and Kittens," *Lounge Art Ensemble,* Music for Moderns

That was done on a Yamaha Cocktail kit, I was always doing stupid shit like that, they were sort of fun to play though. That wasn't a bad cut. I was still only about halfway there in really understanding New Orleans music. It was only later after Hurricane Katrina, when I started paying more attention to things, that I realized that the New Orleans thing was more vertical and more right on the money. When people (like myself) do a bad imitation of New Orleans drumming, it sounds like an actor doing a really bad accent in a movie.

"Hawaii Bathing Suit," Peter Erskine, *Dr. Um*

Ex 26 - The quick tempo of "Hawaii Bathing Suit" is counterbalanced with Erskine's relaxed feel. He uses the hi-hat as a comping voice along with the bass and snare drums. (0:00)

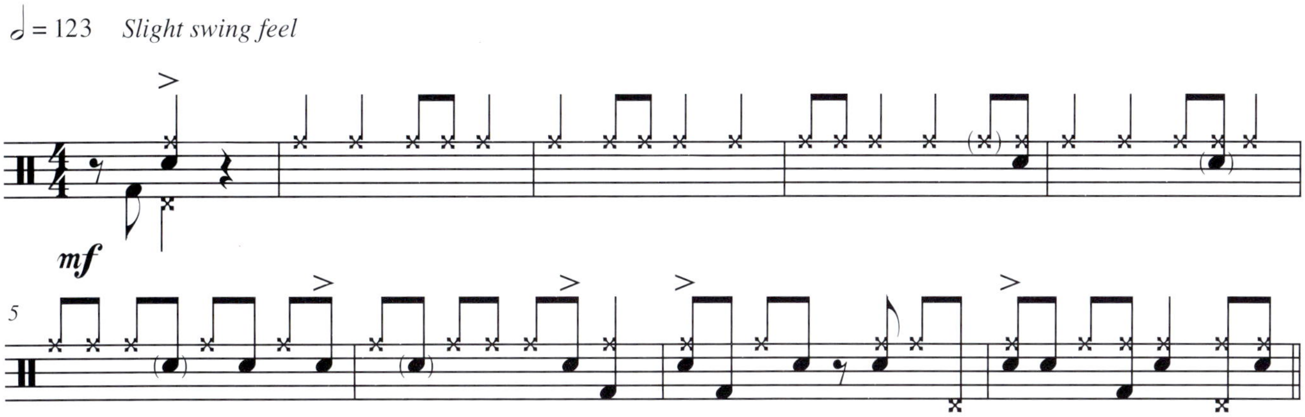

Melody

Ex 27 - In the later part of the melody, he mixes things up by shifting into a calypso beat. (0:39)

Peter's Thoughts on…
"Hawaii Bathing Suit," Peter Erskine, *Dr. Um*

I wrote this tune for a Japanese Theme Park, they hated it! I brought it to one of my ECM recording sessions, and the band and the producer hated it. Then I finally got to record it on *Dr. Um*. It's a calypso with bad intentions.

"Boogie Shuttle Stop," Alan Pasqua, Dave Carpenter, Peter Erskine, *Badlands*

Ex 28 - This excerpt is from the trading section of "Boogie Shuttle Stop". Erskine's ideas flow effortlessly and provide fuel for the conversational exchanges. (2:32)

Peter's Thoughts on…
"Boogie Shuttle Stop," Alan Pasqua, Dave Carpenter, Peter Erskine, *Badlands*

Bassist Dave Carpenter wrote this. We lost Dave way too young. He played with Buddy Rich for several years, and he was the one that told me that he always watched the tip of Buddy's stick on the ride cymbal to help him with the time.

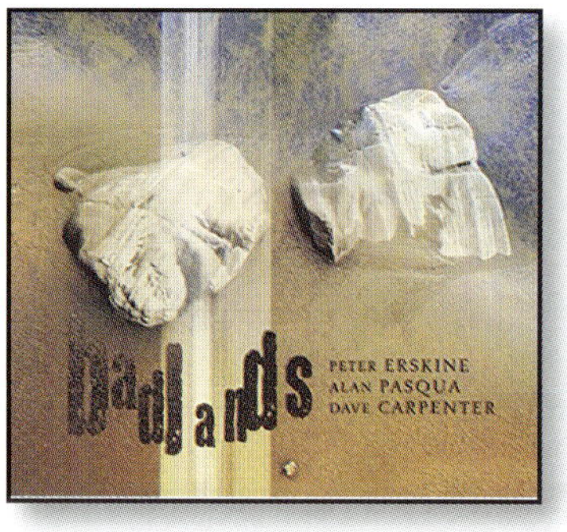

The tune on this album that I liked the most was "Daddy, What is God's Last Name?" I thought that for all of the places that tune *could* have gone drum-wise, I really liked where it *actually* went. Meaning that I liked my self-editing on that tune. These days, at least for me, what gets left out, becomes more interesting than what I played. Because then, when I do add "something" it's more interesting.

"Leroy Street," Peter Erskine, *Peter Erskine*

Ex 29 - Erskine gives a nod to the great Elvin Jones on the swinging mambo feel of "Leroy Street". He incorporates some slick triplet vocabulary at the ends of phrases that add forward motion. (0:27)

Peter's Thoughts on…
"Leroy Street," *Peter Erskine*

Randy Brecker and I wrote this. It is Elvin-esque, and I had Don Alias there to help my chances… at that point I still wasn't understanding Elvin fully.

I heard Adam Nussbaum recently, and I think he does the best "Elvin" of anybody.

But (here's the key,) he "does Elvin" so well because he isn't trying to. Whenever a drummer consciously thinks "I'm going to do my tribute to Elvin," it just doesn't work. Elvin was a huge influence of mine!

"Mr. Fonebone," Jaco Pastorius, *Truth, Liberty, and Soul, Live*

Ex 30 - Peter catches the band's unison syncopated rhythms on the bass drum while the hi-hat and snare drum play an upbeat funk groove on top. (1:25) **note: written in half-time for clarity.*

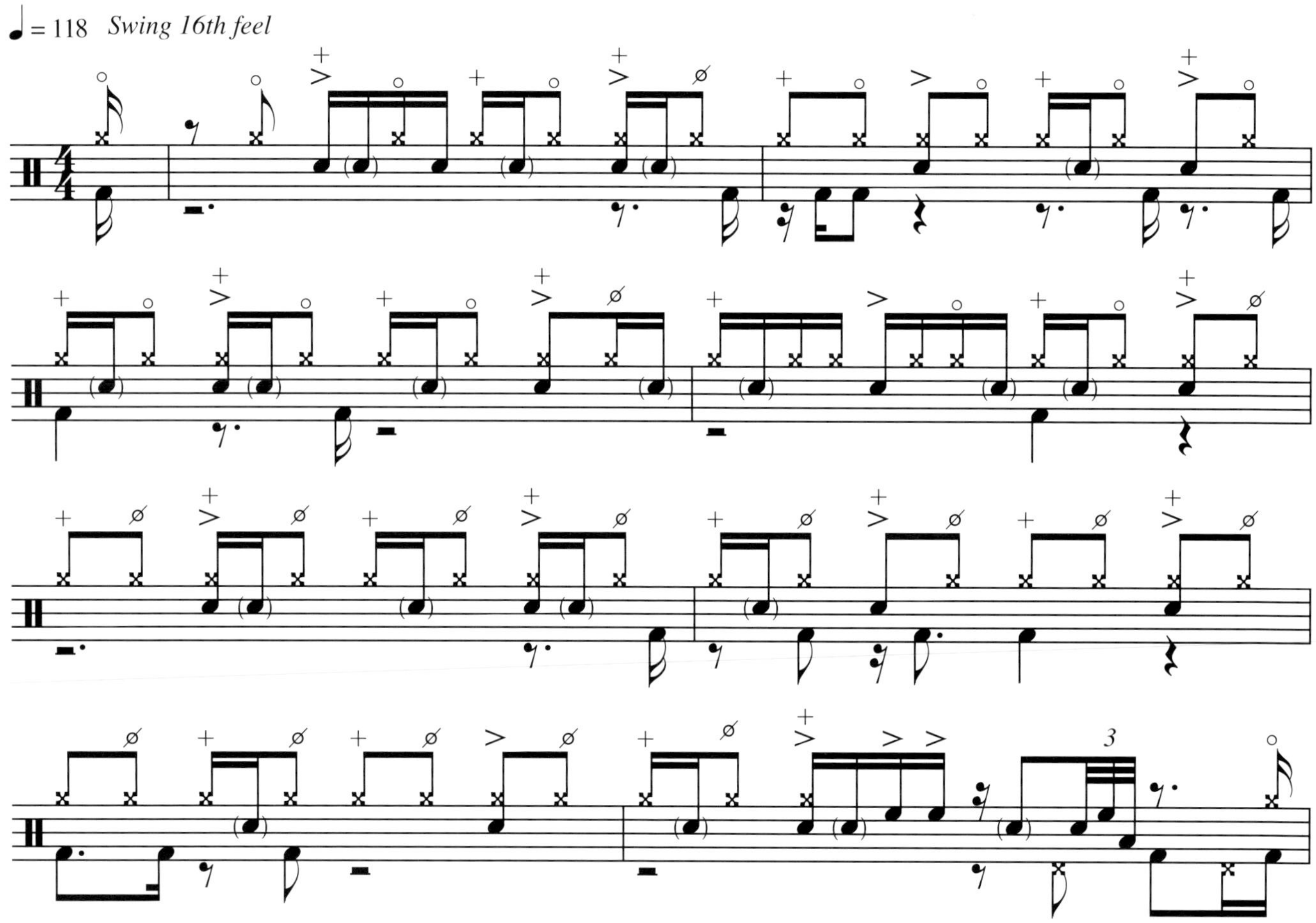

Ex 31 - On the last time through the figures, Erskine lets loose with a solo. He plays over-the-barline phrases that play off of the band's jagged rhythms. (8:37)

Peter's Thoughts on…

"Mr. Fonebone," Jaco Pastorius, *Truth, Liberty, and Soul, Live*

This was the day after I recorded my first solo album. The most memorable thing about that show, was that Jaco called "I Shot the Sherriff" and I had never heard that tune before. He said play reggae, that didn't help much either. So I had to fake the tune on the stage of Lincoln Center.

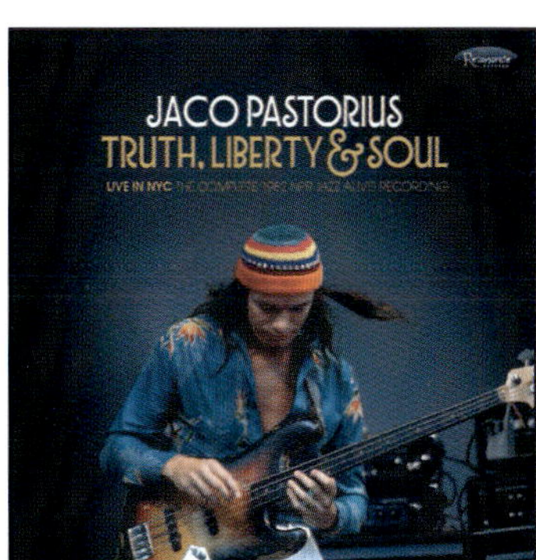

"Furs on Ice," Abercrombie, Johnson, Erskine, *Live*

Ex 32 - The 9/4 meter of "Furs on Ice" is a playground for Peter's loose phrasing concept. He conveys an "anything can happen" energy with his explorative drumming. (0:56)

Peter's Thoughts on...

"Furs on Ice," *Abercrombie, Johnson, Erskine, Live*

That's a hilarious tune, and a great band. Playing with John Abercrombie was a treat. He was one of the most original musicians that I ever got a chance to know, and that tour was a thrill. In our travels together, Marc Johnson and I have talked about music a lot, we have really workshopped what we do together. I probably trust him as much (or more) that any other bass player that I have ever known, you know what I mean?

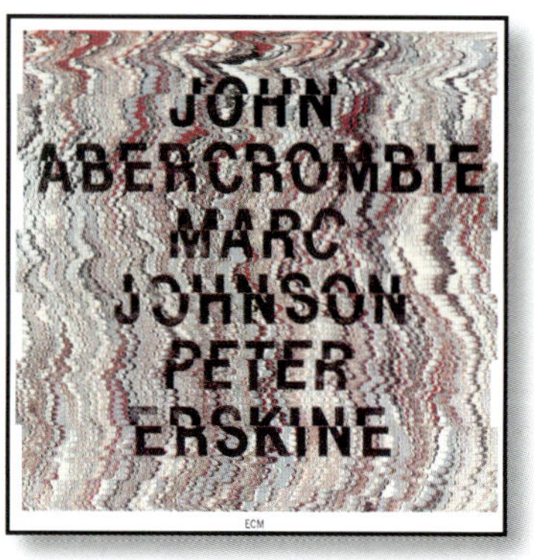

"Friday Night at the Cadillac Club," Bob Berg, *Short Stories*

Ex 33 - Erskine swings hard with a straightforward shuffle on "Friday Night at the Cadillac Club". (0:00)

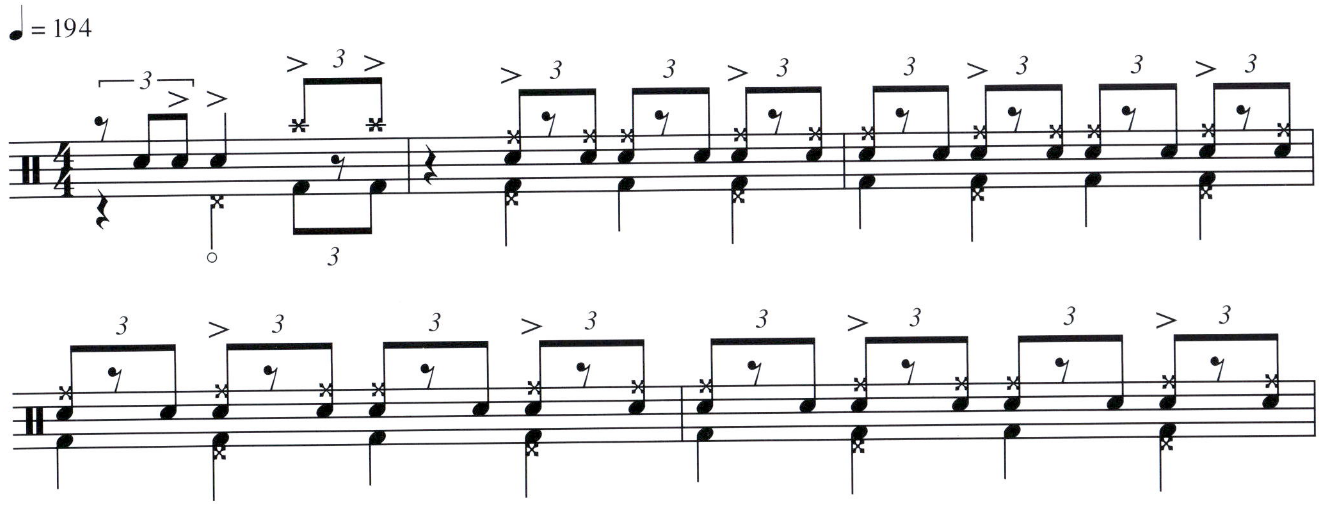

Peter's Thoughts on...
Groove from "Friday Night at the Cadillac Club," Bob Berg, *Short Stories*

That's a great tune, and it's got some energy. I'm going to complete the circle here. When I met Billy Cobham for the first time, it was 1971. I walked up to him and said, "Mr. Cobham I love the way that you played on (Miles Davis') "Jack Johnson!" And Billy turned to me and said, "Shit, it was only a shuffle." So for as much as you (and others) like that tune, I'm going to say, "Thanks. But, shit, it was only a shuffle."

MD: But what a great shuffle it is!

"Erskoman," Peter Erskine, *Motion Poet*

Ex 34 - Peter sets up the quasi-calypso feel of "Erskoman" with a four-on-the-floor bass drum part and cross-stick backbeats on 2 and 4. The hi-hat plays a syncopated rhythm across the solid foundation. (0:00)

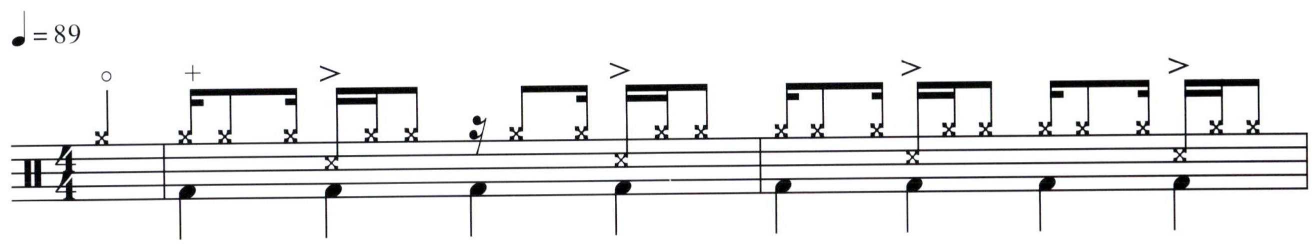

Ex 35 - Later in the song, Peter plays a groovy solo over a bass and percussion vamp. He keeps the pocket in tact while playing interesting ideas around the time. (4:08)

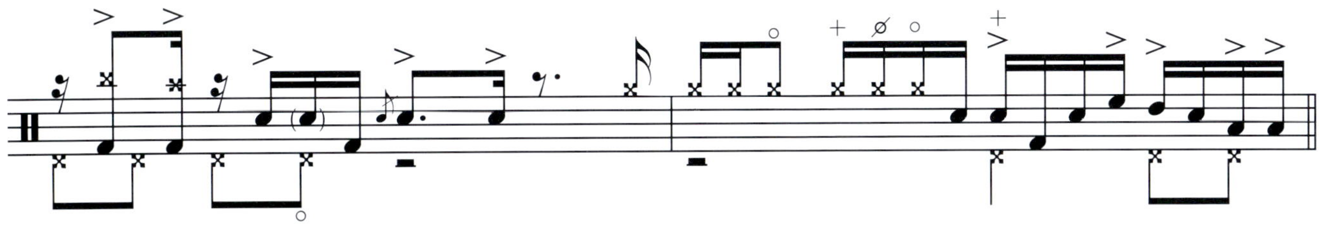

Peter's Thoughts on…
"Erskoman," Peter Erskine, *Motion Poet*

That tune is a riff on Wayne Shorter's tune "Pearl on the Half Shell" from Weather Report *Sportin' Life.* Zawinul told me, "Stop composing in the key of C, try composing in a key you're not too comfortable with." He continued

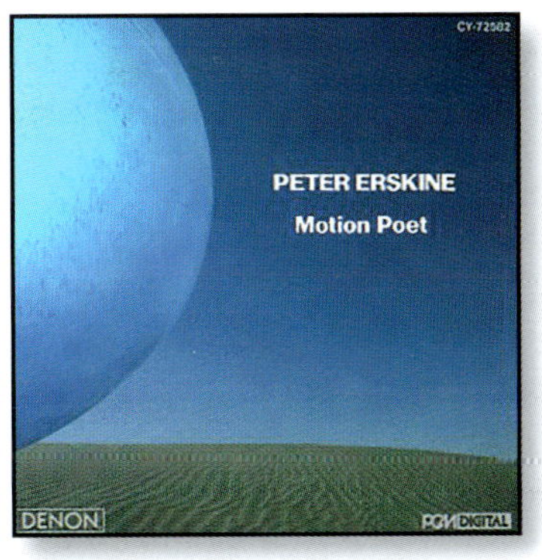

by saying, "If for nothing else, even by accident, you'll come up with some pretty hip chords." So (of course) I went to C sharp. I was very reliant on MIDI sequencing back then for my composing, now I'm much more paper and pencil.

"But is it Art?" Peter Erskine, *Sweet Soul*

Ex 36 - On this drum solo tribute to Art Blakey, Erskine employs rhythmic themes, riffs and melodic motifs to great effect. On this section, he rhythmically transposes a four-note melody on the drums under a steady ride cymbal beat. (0:48)

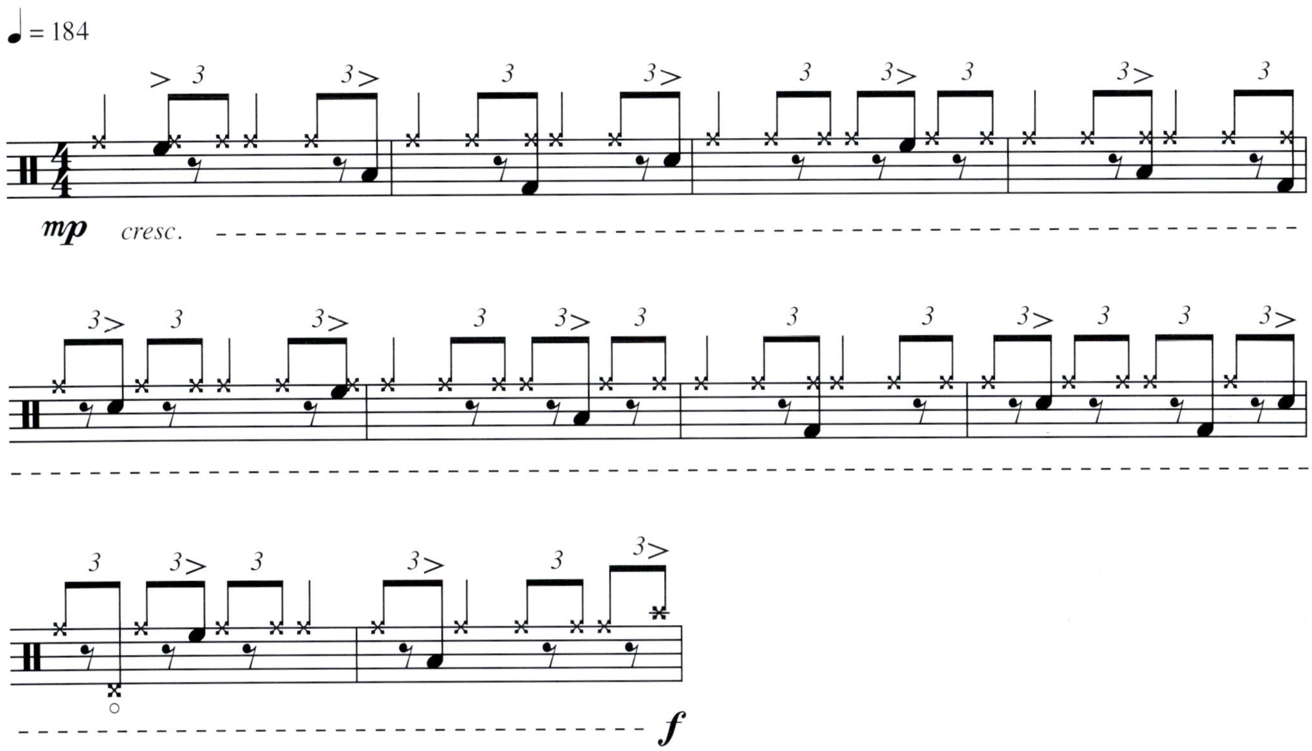

Peter's Thoughts on...
"But is it Art?" Peter Erskine, *Sweet Soul*

Another expression of my conceit by playing a drum solo on a record. The title is a word play on Art Blakey. That entire record was too long. That was when I recorded the William Walton classical composition "Touch Her Soft Lips and Part" and treated it as a jazz tune, and it sort of became a standard, which makes me proud.

I recently recorded a Mahler composition on *Dr. Um* as an experiment. And some reviewer made a snarky remark that was patronizing and condescending along the lines of, "*Ooooh, let's play something classical in a jazz style.*" That really pissed me off!!! Look, we're trying something here. I felt like telling him (and now I will,) "I've been doing this (playing classical music with a jazz approach) for years. I wanted to bring some musical wealth to the community, so we tried something, it was nothing new for me. Too many people are trying to be funny, and not dealing with the **music.**"" That's the kind of reviewing cheap shot that gives critics a bad name. If I want David Letterman, I'll turn on the TV.

"The Aleph," Steps, *Paradox*

Ex 37 - After an intense extended solo, Peter cues the band back in by playing the melody of "The Aleph" on the drums. (18:10)

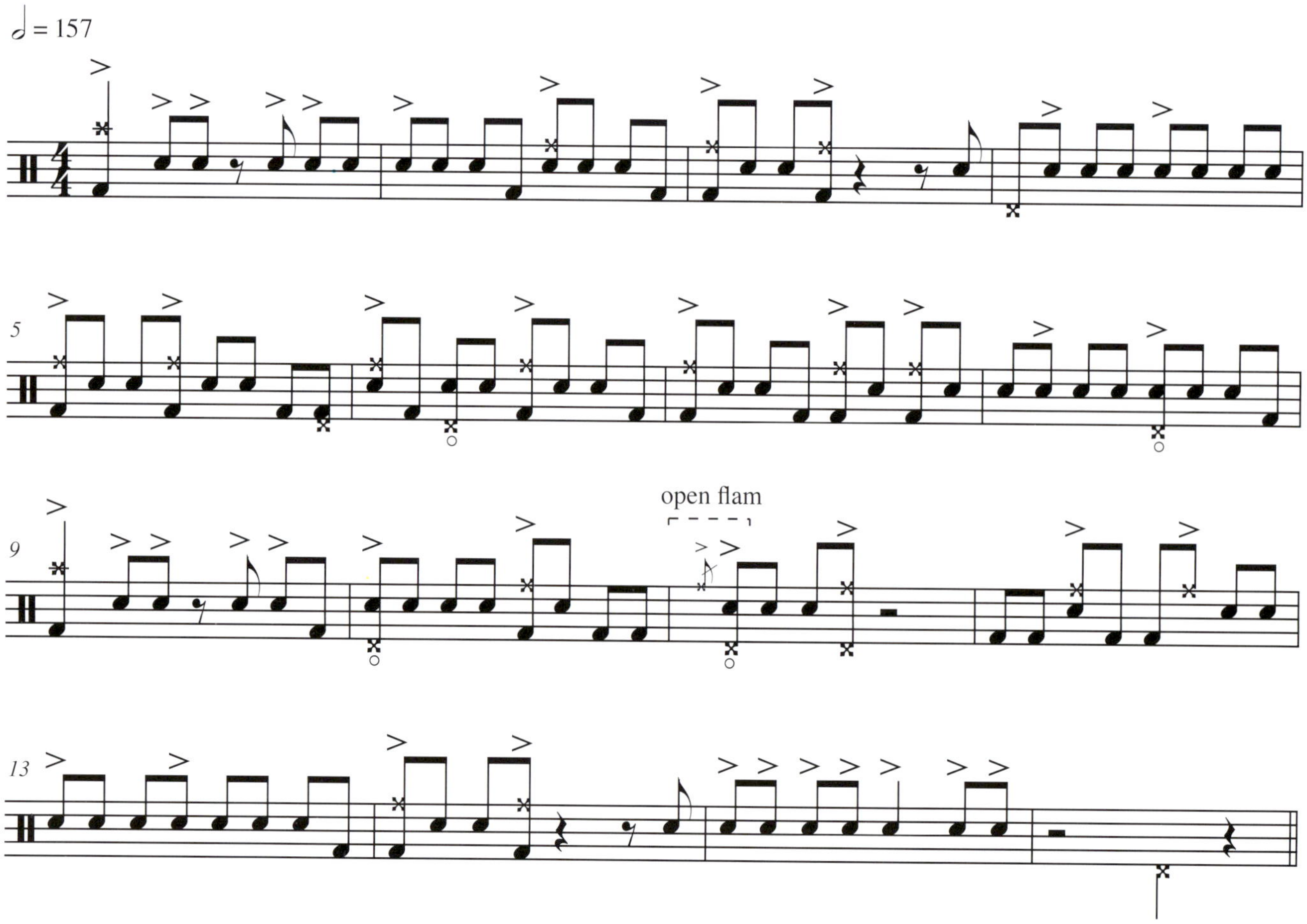

Peter's Thoughts on…

"The Aleph," (drum solo) Steps, *Paradox*

I haven't listened to this in a long time, there's some wonderful playing by the group. The original album version of this had the drum solo edited out (the album was originally released as an LP,) so I'm listening to the "alternate take" CD version. I'm enjoying the sound of that Yamaha drumset! And this alternate take is awfully good. What a privilege it was to be in a band with Michael Brecker, Mike Mainieri, Eddie Gomez and Don Grolnick (and, later, Eliane Elias.) These guys were the reason I moved to New York. Okay, the solo.

Sorry, I'm digging the interactive playing. I remember playing this one time at this same club, Seventh Avenue South, and my drums were set-up on the stage left side of the bandstand. And, while I was playing, drummer Philip Wilson was standing right next to me and checking it out. We exchanged nods and his seemed to be an approving one, and that made me feel really good. Wow, this alternate take is really good. I have to listen to the entire tune so that I hear the drum solo in context. Too bad this was not included on the original album!

Analytically, I'm enjoying the textural density while still being able to hear thematic elements of the tune. It sounds a bit forced here and there, but not bad overall. I think the ride cymbal that I'm playing is from my childhood kit. It measured just under 18" in diameter, this might have been the gig where it cracked and became history.

"Some Skunk Funk," Brecker Brothers and the WDR Big Band, *Some Skunk Funk*

Ex 38 - Erskine shows his funky side on this command performance of the Brecker Brothers' "Some Skunk Funk". He digs into the pocket, and plays the head of the song with power and precision. (0:00)

Ex 39 - He sets the atmosphere of Randy Brecker's solo with a sneaky half-time feel. He brings his auxiliary snare drum in on the second bar of the groove for a double backbeat. (3:19)

Peter's Thoughts on…

"Some Skunk Funk," *Brecker Brothers and the WDR Big Band, Some Skunk Funk*

That tune and performance speaks for itself. Michael Brecker always seemed to be at the height of his powers. Mike had died by the time this was released, and this record — and Mike's solo — received a Grammy Award. But in my opinion EVERY solo that Michael Brecker ever recorded is worthy of a Grammy. Everyone sounds great on that record, by the way.

"Babe of the Day," Vince Mendoza, *Start Here*

Ex 40 - Peter sails through the complex rhythms of "Babe of the Day" with the confidence, commitment and style that only he can deliver. This dense mixed-meter section is a great example of why Erskine gets the call for a heavy session like this. (1:34)

Peter's Thoughts on…

"Babe of the Day," Vince Mendoza, *Start Here*

This made me "famous" in some circles because it's a helluva challenging piece to play. It was not only tough from a reading point of view, but also as far as keeping the ship and the horizon perfectly level. There is a lot happening syncopation-wise. The whole band really worked on and practiced this piece really slowly before recording it. We learned it right there in the studio during the session. No rehearsal.

Peter Erskine Photo Gallery

Peter Erskine Library

Peter Erskine Library

Peter Erskine Library

Photo Gallery

Marco Soccoli

Peter Erskine Library

Peter Erskine Library

Photo Gallery

Marco Soccoli